Coaching by the Book

4055-LEDE

Coaching by the Book

Principles of Christian Coaching

Ruth Ledesma
with Members of the
Christian   Coaches Network

4055-LEDE

To order additional copies of this book, contact:

Ledesma Associates
1-800-355-7552
www.RuthLedesma.com
Orders@RuthLedesma.com

Contents

ACKNOWLEDGEMENTS 11

INTRODUCTION 13

ABUNDANT LIFE 17

SIMPLIFYING LIFE 27

SERVE BY RESERVE 35

EMBRACING THE WHOLE PERSON 45

DEVELOPING GOD'S GIFTS 53

ASSIGNMENTS AND RESTS 61

DRAWING YOUR LINE IN THE SAND: 67

CHOICES 75

COMPLETION: 83

ACCEPTANCE 91

GETTING YOUR LIFE BACK: 101

THE JOY OF COMMUNITY 111

Appendix A 119

Appendix B 121

Appendix C 123

Appendix D 129

Praise for

COACHING BY THE BOOK

"Coaching by the Book sets you on the way to exploring the rich relationship between coaching concepts and Christian teaching. Written specifically for anyone who wants to be coached from a Christian point of view and for coaches who seek a Biblical foundation for their work."
Sandy Vilas, CEO, CoachInc.com

"I was asked to review one chapter of *Coaching By The Book*; but I became so engrossed that, before I knew what had happened, I had read the whole thing! It is a rare find: a book that is not only faithful to the Holy Scriptures, but is also chock-full of wisdom for living, covers all the key areas of life that folk have problems with, *and* is easy to read. A "must buy" in my view, for every Church library, and everyone who wants more out of their lives."
Rev. Dr. John Clements, Author *Make Your Walls Tumble,*
International Speaker and Coach, Norwich, England.

"I especially enjoyed the chapter on abundance. Ruth did a great job of tying together the Biblical references and the practical examples of real people. The client stories illustrate how coaching helps people make these concepts real in their lives. *Coaching by the Book* makes it simple and clear: a nice blend of the spiritual and the practical."
Val Williams, Master Certified Coach,
Professional Coaching and Training, Inc.

4055-LEDE

"Finally! A book about distinctly Christian Coaching by those who practice it and are shaping the field! Not simply traditional coaching fare with a few scriptures peppered throughout, but an examination of the Christian life with the Scriptures as its foundation."

Christopher McCluskey,
President, Coaching for Christian Living

"*Coaching by The Book* exemplifies the values inherent in the Christian faith with a variety of essays written by personal life coaches who emphasize their faith as a way of purposeful living. It teaches without preaching and presents thoughtful guidelines for those in the profession of life coaching for themselves and their clients."

Dr. Patrick Williams, Master Certified Coach
President, Institute for Life Coach Training
(a program of Therapist University)

"*Coaching by the Book* is a great refrence tool for professionals and entrepreneurs. I especially enjoyed the chapters Abundant Life and Simplifying Life. This book provides a Christian prespective that can be integrated into most secular environments. The stories were realistic and enhanced the text. Celebrating and sharing your gifts/talents and appreciating life's simple treasures will help one grow as a contributor and not just as a user of our resources. This book will be on the recommendation list for my clients and associates."

Genevia Gee Fulbright, CPA,
Fulbright & Fulbright, CPA, PA

"... asking God to fill you with the knowledge of his will through all spiritual wisdom and understanding. And we pray this in order that you may live a life worthy of the Lord and may please him in every way: bearing fruit in every good work, growing in the knowledge of God, being strengthened with all power according to his glorious might so that you may have great endurance and patience, and joyfully giving thanks to the Father, who has qualified you to share in the inheritance of the saints in the kingdom of light."

Colossians 1:9-12

ACKNOWLEDGEMENTS

Of primary importance, I am most humbly grateful to God, the Creator and Sustainer, for the gift of the concept for this book and for all the miracles it took to turn it into tangible reality.

From the very beginning, this book has been supported by friends, family and members of the Christian Coaches Network (CCN). I say a heartfelt "thank you" to all those who kept "The Book Crew" in their prayers. In addition, I particularly want to recognize the contributions of the following members of the team:

The Contributors: Carwin Dover, Marilyn O'Hearne, Terry Phillips, Judy Santos, Tim Ursiny, and Gary Wood. Had we waited for me to write the whole book, we would have waited a very long time. These talented coaches have contributed their insights as both coaches and Christians to make this book worthy of consideration by anyone who wants to learn how the coaching profession is supported by Biblical teaching.

Judy Santos: Not only did she write two excellent chapters for the book, she served as a constant source of feedback and creativity in organizing and carrying out this project. As founder and director of CCN, her vision has made possible the collaboration so necessary for completion of this book.

Cecile Adams: Cecile's editing skills have been invaluable in bringing this book to press. She kept us on the path of clarity and also provided an outstanding summary description of an Effective Spiritual Coach.

Brent and Pam King: Professional photographer Brent King and his lovely wife Pam brought their artistic and technical abilities to creating a cover photo that beautifully depicts the integral relationship between the Word of God (represented by a well-used Bible) and Christian coaching (represented by the telephone headset).

Carol Gerrish: Without fail, Carol has supported us with special assignments and special prayers. She has remained faithful throughout the long and sometimes murky process of bringing this project to fruition.

And finally, my heartfelt thanks to the many people who have made coaching the legitimate profession it is today.

Ruth Ledesma

INTRODUCTION

A critical question for you as a practicing Christian should always be "How does . . . relate to Biblical teaching and my values as a Christian?" This question carries even more significance within the coaching relationship, for partnering with a professional coach often leads to major changes in your life over a relatively short period of time. This question, along with an honest answer, becomes the touchstone assuring that those changes will be in accord with God's purpose for your life.

This book is written for anyone who wants to learn more about coaching but is designed to be particularly helpful as a reference for those who want to coach—or be coached—specifically from a Christian perspective. Because coaching is always confidential, the writers have altered case examples or created composite situations to demonstrate how coaching works while still protecting the anonymity of their clients.

When personal and business coaching was introduced in the early 1990's as a profession, the founders intended to make the concepts religion-neutral. In particular, I believe coaching pioneer Thomas Leonard clearly recognized that the principles that support effective coaching are relevant to *all* humanity and believed they transcended any particular religious teaching.

Coaching by the Book essentially translates some of the religion-neutral concepts of coaching into more familiar Christian terminology. (NIV references are used unless otherwise noted.) We want to make it easy to see the correlations. The writers of the various chapters have shown the Biblical support to be found for several of the basic concepts of coaching, but there are many more coaching concepts still expressed in religion-neutral terms. We hope this book will be enough to convince you that the search for a scriptural foundation for *any* coaching concept is worth the effort.

Because the Christian Coaches Network is comprised of people from a wide range of denominations, this book does not necessarily represent the views of all its members. You will notice in reading the book that even the writers have different approaches to their topics. As the author of record, I have tried to allow the true voice of each writer to come through clearly, for I have the deepest respect and appreciation for God's infinite manifestation in the lives of his believers.

Background:

I enrolled in coach training with Coach University in 1997 and quickly found that I, like so many others, had been coaching all my life as a gifted amateur. While there were new ideas enough to delight my personal thirst for growth and development, there were also many ideas with which I had been familiar all my life. Those familiar ideas were solidly rooted in my Christian training and experience. I easily found that Biblical support for the newer ideas was also readily available through the diligent use of my Concordance.

The new ideas and the old quickly blended into a cohesive whole and I became a professional coach, confident that I was serving my clients in a way that reflected my deepest convictions. That continues to be true today for my coaching practice is filled with people of diverse religious faiths who reflect differing levels of spiritual insight.

However, I found myself spending quite a bit of time reassuring my Christian clients and explaining how the coaching concepts relate to Christian teaching. I suppose my concern for this situation, so heavy in my heart, was the reason God gave me the gift of the idea for this book.

One day I was wondering what could be done and the next day the whole book was there in my mind: cover photo, title, and general content—the whole thing. I was burning to write this book and even started on it but quickly foundered. The book sat in a back corner of my mind for what seemed an eternity. Then, following the 1999 conference of the International Coach Federation, other members of the Christian Coaches Network (CCN) expressed the desire to enhance the visibility and credibility of Christian coaching. When I opened the writing of the book to other members of CCN, several willing people came forward with exactly the abilities and the enthusiasm needed to get this book moving at last.

I, and all the wonderful and talented people who have been a part of this endeavor, pass on to you this gift God gave to me. We pray that you and all those whose lives you touch will benefit from what you learn here.

Blessings,
Ruth Ledesma

1 | ABUNDANT LIFE

By Ruth Ledesma

"Whoever loves money never has money enough; whoever loves wealth is never satisfied with his income. This too is meaningless."
Ecclesiastes 5:10

"And do not set your heart on what you will eat or drink; do not worry about it. For the pagan world runs after all such things, and your Father knows that you need them. But seek his kingdom, and these things will be given to you as well."
Luke 12:29-31

"Grace and peace be yours in abundance through the knowledge of God and of Jesus our Lord."
2 Peter 1:2

"The Lord is good, a refuge in times of trouble. He cares for those who trust in Him."
Nahum 1:7

"Delight yourself in the Lord and he will give you the desires of your heart."
Psalm 37:4

"Remember this: Whoever sows sparingly will also reap sparingly, and whoever sows generously will also reap generously. Each man should give what he has decided in his heart to give, not reluctantly or under compulsion, for God loves a cheerful giver. And God is able to make all grace abound to you, so that in all things at all times, having all that you need, you will abound in every good work. As it is written:

'He has scattered abroad his gifts to the poor; his righteousness endures forever.'

"Now he who supplies seed to the sower and bread for food will also supply and increase your store of seed and will enlarge the harvest of your righteousness. You will be made rich in every way so that you can be generous on every occasion, and through us your generosity will result in thanksgiving to God."

2 Corinthians 9:6-11

What do most people think of when they consider the term "abundance"? Worldly possessions of some kind tend to come to mind first. Money first, then house, car, computer, and other possessions are listed, along with the job that brings in the money and provides the means to buy all the rest. After wealth, people will usually start listing the treasured people in their lives: spouse, parents, children, friends, etc. When their thinking expands further, the resources of this culture and planet are considered.

One can easily see that, from a material standpoint, we all are limited. Our society teaches so clearly that there just "isn't enough to go around." The phrases in common usage include "Get my share"—because one believes there is not enough to go around; "Dog eat dog" and "It's a jungle out there"—reflecting the belief that one has to fight to survive at the expense of others. And so we build the scarcity mentality rather than one of abundance.

The problem with scarcity mentality is that it focuses on worldly things that indeed can come and go much faster than we might like, worldly things that really may not be sufficient to meet the needs of all the people of the world and can be depleted to the point of nonexistence. Who can refute the poverty that binds so many people in our world? Who can refute the millions of children starving to death every day? Who can refute the disappearance of the ozone layer, fossil fuels, the rainforest, etc.?

The Bible calls us, however, to make God the center of our lives. The Bible is filled with reference after reference to God's infinite power, to His everlasting love for His children, to His abundant generosity, and to His promises to care for us always and in every way. Clearly we are only required to accept Jesus as our Savior and God as the source of our being and everything else. We simply need to obey His teachings and remember that, because He is infinite, His ability to supply our needs and the desires of our hearts is also infinite. Not only can God provide all the material things we could ever want, but also the far more important peace and joy we want and need to fill our hearts and our lives.

Jeff's Story

Jeff was very successful in his work as a software developer. He had been with his present company since its inception two years ago. His stock options alone had multiplied in value tremendously. Jeff was extremely capable and eager for more responsibility. Promotions, bonuses, and increases in salary were frequent events in his life. He came to coaching because he wanted to accelerate his progress even more.

As we talked about strategies he was already using to enhance his effectiveness, I learned that Jeff was working close to 80 hours per week. He wore his pager 24/7, and his laptop was with him wherever he went, "just in case." There were times he slept on the floor near his desk because he was too tired to go back to his apartment to rest. His diet was replete with pizza, burgers and fries: cooking or even dining out at a traditional restaurant took too much time. His social life was nonexistent: his interactions were only with co-workers as they worked feverishly on the next development.

When I asked about why he was working so intensely, Jeff was sure about two things. First, he truly enjoyed his job and clearly was very well suited for the work. He couldn't imagine any other kind of work giving him the sense of satisfaction he felt when a program he was working on was successful. In this sense, Jeff was truly blessed; and together we celebrated his being in a line of work so well suited to his skills and interests.

The second belief, however, was a major problem. Jeff had bought into the message of affluence. He believed that he needed huge amounts of money to be able to support a family and to live adequately in his later years. He believed if he just worked long and hard he could have enough money to fund the lifestyle he wanted. The word "abundance" meant money and possessions; and he saw only one way for him to get them—long, hard work.

During coaching Jeff devised and implemented time management techniques that worked well for him. He came to a clearer understanding of the value of self-care in enhancing his productivity. He began to order in more nutritious food, and he set up a "cot room" at work where he and others could sleep a bit more comfortably. However he had no success in implementing any strategy that would take time from work. He could not bring himself to start exercising regularly. The idea of taking time off to reconnect with friends outside of work was unthinkable. For Jeff, "down time" was not an acceptable option.

As we began to explore more deeply his reasons for being so very tied to his work, we looked at the concept of "enough." Jeff easily defined what possessions he felt he needed to live comfortably and recognized that multiple cars and homes were an extravagance for which he had no taste. In fact, Jeff already had just the car and apartment he wanted, but no time to enjoy them. He recognized that, in the view of most people, he even had more than enough money to support a family.

Jeff demonstrated the coaching maxim that the client always has the answers (even though he may not realize it) when he finally blurted out, "There's never enough money."

Without the big bank accounts Jeff envisioned, he felt vulnerable to all the problems he identified with poverty. His fear of poverty was driving him mercilessly. He had believed that if he had enough money he would be safe, but now he realized there would never be enough money to do that for him. Jeff made a list of all the phrases he could remember which tied safety to money and who had spoken those words. He was unable to remember any terms that didn't tie the two together, so instead we talked about where a sense of safety could come from, if not from money. Jeff was sure that he felt safe at work and found it quite difficult to list other times in his life when he had felt safe, but was finally able to come up with times as a child when he had felt safe in his mother's arms and with his father. It was a short step to re-examining his ideas about the source of all provision and safety.

Jeff agreed to an in-depth Biblical study of the concept of abundance and God's provision. Although he was in tears at the next coaching call, his voice reflected immense joy. He was finally free of an incredibly heavy burden. Jeff could now rest at last in the understanding that God provides all things in abundance for his children, including Jeff. We continued our coaching around the relationship that is integral to that safety he had craved.

The ultimate result was that Jeff came up with another life plan. His plan included the exercise and other physical self-care he knew he needed. He also included time every day to get out of the office and be a part of this wonderful creation God had given for his pleasure. Walks in the park were routine, and he set aside time to enjoy being in his lovely home. He committed to making at least one social contact per week outside of work and was delighted to re-connect with old friends and family. Most importantly, he scheduled church involvement into his life. He was surprised, but very happy, to find his productivity at work jumped significantly when he brought more balance into his life.

When we last talked, Jeff was dating a delightful young woman from his Bible Study group. His personal turnaround and the rich blessings he is experiencing are a direct result of his opening his heart and his life to our loving God, the source of all that is good in our lives. Jeff has come to agree with one of my personal slogans: "You don't have to do it all to have it all."

Alice's Story

Alice wore secondhand clothes from the Thrift Shop where she worked and lived in a tiny, barren apartment with little furniture and inadequate heating. She was obviously someone who was intimately familiar with poverty.

I got to know her when we were working together, sorting clothes to send to flood victims in our state. We talked about many things, including her great compassion for those whose lives had been so sorely disrupted by the flooding. I learned, by a slip of her tongue, that Alice had gone to several other thrift shops and secondhand stores and bought clothing to donate to this effort. I was amazed, to say the least.

With gentle questioning, I found that Alice had a rather large savings account from which she would occasionally withdraw money for just this kind of charitable project. Most of the money in the account she had inherited from an aunt, and she added to the savings account from each paycheck she received from the Thrift Shop. Alice had never used any of the money for herself and made every effort to view the money as not being hers. It became very clear that she feared being "rich" would exclude her from God's favor and ultimately from heaven.

As an experienced counselor, I could see that Alice's view of money bordered on the pathological. However, I had a hunch her view was based more on an unclear understanding of Biblical teaching than on pathology, so I asked permission to coach her. With her agreement, we began to explore the foundations for her beliefs.

Alice wrote out all her beliefs about money, wealth, riches, abundance, poverty, blessings, gifts, charity, giving and more. Then we joined in a concordance search of the Bible on those same topics. Soon Alice had a solid Biblical foundation for her views. She saw that for all her life she had associated poverty with Godliness. She had believed living "so tight that it hurts" was the right thing to do as a Christian. She had always accepted giving to others as a Godly thing to do, but never considered that God might want to bless her as well.

Alice was sad, to say the least, that she had spent so many years living in unnecessary hardship but resolved that she would no longer throw God's gifts "back in His face." She decided to move into a more comfortable apartment with central heating and air conditioning; and she furnished it with some good, used pieces. She still buys clothes at the thrift shop, but now she shops the sales for a few new clothes as well. Her grocery bill has gone up because she is eating more nutritious food.

Yet Alice is still living within her income and has no desire for what she refers to as "ostentation." Her latest study topic is personal investing, for she realizes that the money in her savings account has the potential for helping a great many more people if she takes responsibility for it and implements policies of good stewardship.

Alice smiles a lot these days, and not just to show off her new dentures. She keeps a gratitude journal. Each evening she writes at least one page in her journal, listing the things for which she is grateful. Her coaching and study have resulted in a deeper, more loving relationship with God; and her face and her life show that.

Conclusion

The key is to focus on building a solid relationship with God. With that relationship as the primary consideration, the faithful, trusting, "righteous man" or woman recognizes that wealth and worldly possessions are for him/her simply a by-product of that relationship, some of the infinite variety of gifts God chooses to bestow on those He loves so much. The Godly man and woman seek the Giver, not the gifts, and ultimately receive both Giver and gifts according to God's infinite love.

"Rejoice in the Lord always. I will say it again: Rejoice! Let your gentleness be evident to all. The Lord is near. Do not be anxious about anything, but in everything, by prayer and petition, with thanksgiving, present your requests to God. And the peace of God which transcends all understanding, will guard your hearts and your minds in Christ Jesus.

"Finally . . . whatever is true, whatever is noble, whatever is right, whatever is pure, whatever is lovely, whatever is admirable— if anything is excellent or praiseworthy—think about such things."
Philippians 4:4-8

Coaching Moments

- How can we meet our needs through our own power?
- Where does our security really come from?
- What is "enough" for you?
- Are "poor in spirit" and "poor in material things" the same?
- Where does scarcity mentality originate?
- Where does abundance mentality originate?
- How does God want us to see Him and our lives in terms of abundance or scarcity?

Coaching Challenges

- Write down all the phrases you remember about money and its purpose.

- Beside each phrase, write the name of the person you have heard use the phrase the most often.
- Use a biblical concordance to study the words from steps 1 and 2 most relevant to your beliefs?
- What do you really believe about the God described in the Bible?
- How can you step out in faith that God will provide for you in abundance?
- How can you accept God's gifts with joy and thanksgiving and still keep your focus on the Giver?

2 | SIMPLIFYING LIFE

By Carwin Dover

"Simplifying" is a bit of an oxymoron in a society where everyone wants more. How can God's principle of "more equals less" apply to your life?

"Ah, to have the simple life." Many have said it. Few would say they have it. Many want it. Few seem to live it.

My first experience with coaching included researching the coaching process and finding a coach. Each article, web site and coach I interviewed mentioned the value of "Simplifying Life." None of them quoted scripture, but their theme was certainly scriptural!

Jesus promised a more simple life. *"Come to me, all you who are weary and burdened, and I will give you rest . . . For my yoke is easy and my burden is light." (Matthew 11: 28-30)*

My early coaching experience included "de-cluttering", saying "No!", starting new habits, and giving up older complicated ones. One coach I interviewed warned me about becoming a coach. "You won't succeed until you do it," she said, referring to the basic coaching principle of living a simple life.

A second idea given me about living a simple life was hiring a coach for life. As I gave pause to this idea, I remembered we humans are lacking in long-term memory when it comes to maintaining good habits. After all, why do we do better when we go to church every Sunday? Why is life a little bit better when we visit with God every day? "Maybe having a coach for life does make sense!" I thought.

So how do people live a more simple life? What does it look like? What does it feel like? Is a simple life more attractive when living it than when not living it?

My goal is to keep the following commentary simple!

It is a way for me to simplify my life.

First, consider the outrageous possibility that a simple life style is more than a principle of God's. It is a gift from God. If a gift, then part of the "How?" is already in place. Good News!

Second, observe people around you who now have a simple life. If others can do it, maybe there is hope for you, too! You can learn from them.

Third, plan how you can prepare yourself for God's gift of simplicity when it is (or has been) given to you.

Simplicity: A Gift from God!

I suspect simplicity is not a gift that God withholds from us until He decides it is time. Instead, I suspect that simplicity is a gift that is discovered over time. It is there for the taking. All you have to do is open it. An early death might preclude some from experiencing the gift of simplicity, but I think the gift is always there—waiting to be opened. Your coach can help you find it and open it sooner than you might if left to your own approach.

Let me tell you a short story I once heard about unopened, under-appreciated gifts. (The original author is unknown.)

There was a baby girl born in a family with a Mom and Dad and a very proud Grandma. This little girl was very blessed because she also had a brother who prepared her parents for the trials of raising kids. There were also several other family members including grandparents, aunts, uncles and an assortment of cousins.

Birthdays and Christmas were special events. Mary, the little girl, squealed with delight when the time came to open the presents. Paper ripped and ribbons flew. Mary's parents worked hard to keep track of who gave what.

After Mary turned 5, she began to notice one package that was always the same: No fancy ribbon or paper. And inside was another one of those old handkerchiefs from Grandma. "What a boring gift! Why does she keep giving me something I don't want? If I wanted to, Mom wouldn't let me use it. So what's the use? Grandma has the money. Why doesn't she give me something I really want?"

Mary had difficulty saying, "Thank you, Grandma" while thinking those thoughts. She knew that her Mom would insist on her thanking Grandma, so, out slid the monotone, "Thank you for the handkerchief, Grandma."

Year after year, the same old thing happened: another hand-kerchief from Grandma. "Too bad she doesn't have any imagination!"

As Mary grew, she found her collection increasing even faster with such events as her music recital, Confirmation, high school graduation, college graduation. Yes, even her wedding gift was a handkerchief from Grandma!

A few years went by, and Mary received a call at work one day from Mom. "Grandma died today. Come home if you can."

The timing was bad. Mary was eight months pregnant, and travel would be hard. But Mom insisted. "Grandma always loved you, Mary. You were a favorite of hers."

"She never showed it much," Mary thought. "She was always there, but she never said much. All she could ever give me was the same old handkerchief for everything. At least I won't have to get a bigger box now . . . . Hmmm. That's a bit harsh! Grandma didn't mean to be boring. I'll go for Mom and pay my last respects," Mary said to herself.

The big day arrived: Sarah's first birthday! The family had gathered, and Mary was a bit nervous about how much cake her one-year-old daughter would scatter.

After the party, Mom was helping Mary clean up. Mary noticed Mom was especially quiet and was fighting back tears.

"What's wrong? You're supposed to be having fun!"

"It just hit me, Mary. Your Grandma gave me a handkerchief

before she died and asked me to give it to your daughter on her first birthday."

"She never gave up, did she?" exclaimed Mary.

"What do you mean?"

"All she ever gave me was the same old gift." Mary was showing a bit of disappointment. "I always wished she had given me something a little more fun, or at least a little creative."

Astounded, Mom said, "You never really looked at those handkerchiefs, did you?"

A chord suddenly struck Mary. "What do you mean? They were all the same—plain, old, white handkerchiefs. Look for yourself. They are right in here in this box."

The lid opened easily. Mary reached in and grabbed a handful of soft cloth. Then, for the first time, she looked closely. Each border was a little different. On some, a date was barely visible, gently and carefully included in the intricate handwork of her Grandma's. Slowly, for the first time, Mary began to take in the value of her Grandma's gifts.

"Oh . . . I never noticed before. Each one is different. How could I have missed it? I never really said thank you . . . ."

Each year, each birthday, each Christmas, and every other special event, Sarah received one "special" gift from her Mom who said something about this being a gift from Sarah's Great Grandma. But what's so special about a dumb handkerchief you can't use?

God's gift of simplicity is easily unnoticed. His sacrifice is not blatantly evident. Only in a moment of quiet resignation is it possible to begin to take in the enormity and value of simplicity.

What would have happened if Mary's mom had used a coaching approach earlier in her life? "What do you see when you look at the handkerchief?" "What else?" and "What else?" Mary would have been encouraged to look deeper to discover the real gift. That's one of the things a coach does.

Simplicity—Observe: There are people who live it.

Spend some time with someone over 85. Notice their routine. Notice their diet. Notice their spending habits. Notice their response to visitors.

Age has a way of inviting a person to accept the gift of simplicity. Spending time with such a person is an opportunity to begin to appreciate a simple lifestyle.

Illness and injury make simplicity attractive, too. When the effort to be complicated is too much, God's gift can seem to be a generous option. Worry, frustration, anger, and depression are also alternatives; but remember that they are not the gift God gives at such moments. His gift of simplicity is an option to solve a problem. He includes ample opportunity to relate to Him as well. It seems like the more simplicity one adds the more time one has for Him! He suggests that slow is okay . . . less is more . . . last is first.

I had the privilege of having my parents live with us in their last few years. My first adjustment was matching my Dad's pace when he walked. At first I hated it. As time went on, I grew to love it. I saw more, heard more; and, most of all I could finally keep up with him!

Walking with effort never seemed attractive to me before. Now I admire and respect the fight to live. Simplicity is a gift that makes it possible to continue the race. Had I been experiencing this with a coach, I think I would have learned more quickly. My coach would have asked such things as, "What is your Dad's pace teaching you?" "What else?" "What else?" I wonder how much more I would have learned about simplicity if I had learned more quickly with a coach?

Simplicity—Plan: Prepare to receive it.

The odds are in your favor. Today's nutrition, healthcare, and safety inventions give you the chance to live to be physically old. You can hate it. You can fight it. But if you live long enough, simplicity will have its way with you.

My Dad gardened until he was 95. Try as he might to do more, he did less. When he did less anyway and did what he could, he did more! I still maintain the roses and flower beds he started in his nineties.

God made a promise. He said that if you will let Him be first, ahead of anything or anyone else, you will receive more in abundance than if you do it on your own. Look around at what happens when you take over. Immediately, it gets complicated! You do more and achieve less.

Listen to His promise. Believe His promise. Live His promise.

Your Christian coach will probably encourage you to make goals to live more simply, to live in search of God's gift of simplicity. Making life simple is not about being selfish or lazy. Making life simple is truly about serving, being thankful and receiving one of God's gifts graciously.

Coaching Moments

- Give yourself some quiet time. Soak up the simplicity of just being alive. You may think you are doing nothing. Assume you are doing everything you need to do for the moment. Listen. Say nothing. What is the experience like for you? It may take many attempts to learn how to have a minute or two of pure silence. Be patient. Simplicity is harder than it looks!
- What do you think it will be like to share your experience of simplicity? Have you noticed that people seem to want it, yet live complicated lifestyles in their attempt to achieve simplicity?
- What are five ways you can simplify your life in the next two weeks?
- What will your life be like when you have begun to simplify it?
- What do you plan to do after you have simplified your life?
- What other choices do you have if a roadblock guides you

in another direction? What are 10 other choices you have for each of the top five priorities you have?

Coaching Challenges

- Assume "simplicity" is a gift.
- What can you do to prepare yourself to receive the gift?
- Why do you think Jesus would want to grant your request?
- What will your life begin to look like as you simplify it?
- What surprises might you receive? Sometimes the areas of your life you think are okay are the very ones God asks you to change! Be sure to look at them too.
- List 10 activities in your life that keep your lifestyle complicated. Which ones do you think will benefit you most if you eliminate them from your life? Which ones may benefit you if you make some minor adjustments to them? What adjustments can you make?
- List 10 ways your relationship with God will improve by giving up the complicated patterns in your life. What benefits might He receive?
- What attracts you to a complicated life? What is the promise you hear? What discoveries do you usually find? What will help you resist the urge to fall into the same trap again once you simplify your life?
- The process of simplifying life is unending. Clutter seems to accumulate under the best of situations. What signals can you notice that will help the process of simplifying happen sooner rather than later? What exercises can you add to your life that will help you maintain a simple life?

3 | SERVE BY RESERVE

By Gary Wood

What is a reserve?

Having a reserve means you have something kept back for future use, something extra. You are not demanding more than you have available. It means you are ready to meet any daily need or emergency that demands those resources. Reserves do not imply that we don't give life our all. It does imply that God made us capable of managing ourselves in such a way that our availability to the Lord is not cut short by our own lack of understanding of the resources that God made available to us.

A good biblical example comes from Joseph's measures to provide for a coming famine in Egypt. *"Let Pharaoh appoint commissioners over the land to take a fifth of the harvest of Egypt during the seven years of abundance. They should collect all the food of these good years that are coming and store up the grain under the authority of Pharaoh, to be kept in the cities for food. This food should be held in reserve for the country, to be used during the seven years of famine that will come upon Egypt, so that the country may not be ruined by the famine." (Genesis 41:35, 36)*

What kinds of reserves are there?

A random list of 18 reserves mentioned by some of my clients is below. Notice how diverse they are. You and I might add other areas to it, unique to each one of us.

- **Discretionary time:** Having lots of time to stop, think, relax or do what you want.
- **Assistance:** Having more than enough people in place so you never ever have to ask for it.
- **Rest:** Getting the kind of sleep and relaxation that your body and soul specifically need.
- **Stability:** Having a completely stable home and work environment around you.
- **Momentum:** Having more than enough positive, forward and motivational motion.
- **Personal Quiet Time:** Never, ever having to rush your time alone with the Lord.
- **Structure:** You have a framework for living so you always know where you are.
- **Money:** Having more than enough, so money, bills and the future are never a worry.
- **Information:** You always have access to all the information you need, when needed.
- **Love:** Your daily life is full of rich, real, caring and mutual relationships.
- **Physical Space:** Expansive and energizing areas always surround you.
- **Emotional Energy:** You receive more than you give out, always having a joyful soul.
- **Physical Energy:** You have all the physical get up and go you need, and more.
- **Prayer Time:** Other than in an emergency, your prayer time never gets bumped for anything.
- **Opportunities:** You have created a pool of opportunity of fulfilling things to do.

- **Wisdom:** You have 24-hour access to wise, godly people and resources around you.
- **Outdoor Environment:** Never a day goes by when you don't enjoy the outdoors.
- **Stimulating Surroundings:** You surround yourself with things that energize you.

These people know that having sufficient and extra of these elements would enable them to be secure and to have choices instead of always trying to scramble to make up what's missing.

Finding extra discretionary time gave Phil time to relax. Hiring in extra assistance gave Terry opportunity to meet with clients and serve them even better. Establishing extra money reserves relieved Anna from the guilt and consequences of late payments.

As children most of us enjoyed reserves of things like time, rest and assistance. Some things like money didn't worry us. Others took care of that for us. Most would love to regain the childlike reserves that made them able to explore life, see what they really were capable of achieving and enjoy it to the fullest. It is more possible than most people think.

We need reserves to be our best

Having a reserve means we don't have to keep being distracted and drained by the need. Rather, we will eliminate problems and pressure and have the unencumbered ability to reach our potential best. Imagine a well. If it has just a little water in it, what happens? You start being very careful with using the water you have. You keep checking the level. You may start worrying. You constantly search for emergency sources. Now imagine the well filled to the top with water. Notice how you feel. Our lives can be like that almost empty well. We live beyond the limits of what we have on hand. There is little left to draw from.

Phil's Story

Consider Phil, struggling to juggle work and family. Phil wanted things to be done right. He'd give 110 percent to any project he put his hand too. He was noticed. More projects and offers of promotion came his way. His experience and expertise were sought out. You'd think this success would energize him, but the opposite took place. Phil's discretionary time eroded. Since work *had* to be done, his family had reluctantly slipped into the discretionary category. Phil had little time for his family, little time to spend with God, no time for himself and constantly lived in the future, longing for a day when it would be different.

Several trips to the hospital later, with panic attacks, missed work and a deteriorating approach to people around him, I received Phil's call. Over time we strategized about the future he saw and how to bring it into the present. Phil needed to carve out some time to actually relax and figure out where he was going. After gaining some real clarity about his tendency towards being a perfectionist, he started by saying "no" to new projects until he finished a project already started. He cut the number of projects back to reflect a more comfortable working pace. This moved him closer to balance.

Phil began praying more and he physically started booking his family in as priority time. He concentrated whole undistracted days on unfinished business, cleaning up his long to-do lists. Bits of discretionary time started to appear. This gave him a little time to relax and think about the offers coming in and just what he and his family really wanted from life. Clarity led to an intentional, but flexible strategy being developed to cover the short, medium and longer terms in his life.

What did Phil get that was so important? Time. Once that was carved out, he could think clearer, act smarter and begin to enjoy his wife, family and himself again. Having a reserve of time improved how he looked at people, his health and his approach to living. Talking about it garnered the respect of others around him. Now, things have changed. No offer or activity could convince Phil to deteriorate that reserve of personal time he now guards so closely.

Remember how God used Elijah as he confronted the prophets of Baal. He was running in emotional high gear. The experience was victorious and successful but very draining emotionally. Then, so soon after, he had literally run for his life in the face of Jezebel threatening to kill him. After such a high, facing the prophets, Elijah had now reached a depressing low. Drained of energy and resources, what did God do?

He supplied Elijah with food, sleep, assistance and a friend. (1 Kings 18,19) Elijah could return to operating at his best. We need reserves to be our best, at work, at home or in ministry. Let's establish initially that the source of that supply is God. It was the case with Phil. It was so with Elijah and it is so with us.

Two key attitudes toward reserves

Our Lord said that he had come so that we could have "life to the full." In Paul's first letter to Timothy he reminded him to let certain people know that God *"provides everything for our enjoyment."* and that they should be *"rich in good deeds, and to be generous and willing to share."* He noted that these dual attitudes of enjoying what you are given and reinvesting what you are given would actually accrue *"treasure . . . as a firm foundation for the coming age"* so that they could *"take hold of the life that is truly life." (1 Tim. 6:17-19)* The Bible says God provides everything for our enjoyment so that we may reinvest for Him. That will allow you and me to experience life the way He meant it to be, abundant and satisfying.

Capacity

We have no capacity to hold and handle anything for God until we come into relationship with Him. We are so used to grasping and holding everything for ourselves, that unless our mind is renewed in this area, getting more of anything can become a selfish pursuit devoid of God and any understanding of how we can enjoy His greater good in our lives. (See Romans 12:2) We need to ask God daily in prayer to increase our capacity to hold what He actually wants to give us.

Having a reserve of anything is a choice. You can use up what you have and wait for more to come along, although some things, like health, sometimes cannot be recovered. That's OK if that is the way you want to live. At times it may be considerably more stressful, but it is your choice. However, you don't have to live that way. There is another way.

Two ways to get a reserve

Require less. Find ways to cut back on the things that are pushing you to have more. You use less water, so you require less from the well. Remember Phil? Requests from others kept pushing him to perform. The pressure to get some time to himself rose to dangerous levels. Other well-meaning people controlled his life. He cut back on the number of projects to which he said yes.

Get more. Identify ways to increase your ability to find, obtain and handle more. You dig a deeper well. Phil changed the way he looked at his family. He'd always known that time with his wife and kids was most important but he'd never let his day planner reflect that. Phil increased his ability to have more personal time by taking care of his family who he had struggled to find time for. Spending focused time on work, and dedicated time for family actually created personal time for Phil.

Phil cut back on saying yes to every request and increased his dedicated time for family. It created a reserve of time for him.

Terry cut back on being involved in every detail of decision-making and increased delegation and staffing to handle detail. It created a reserve of assistance for him.

Anna cut back on personal spending, rearranged payments and increased a reserve account, strategic investing and careful tracking. It created a reserve of money and financial security for her.

When we need resources to draw from, the Lord keeps saying, *"I have the resources you need. Come to me, learn of me, follow me and I will give . . . ."* He has given *"everything we need for life and godliness." (2 Peter 1:3-8)* But, getting a reserve requires that we maintain dependence on God. And being dependent on Him means that whatever we have, energy, health, money, things, time, gifts, they are to be available for God to use as he sees fit.

Christians are much like reservoirs with an inlet and outlet through which God's blessings flow. If there is no control at one end to conserve and reserve what has come in, that water simply flows through with limited benefit available, if it is put to use at all. But, build a dam at the outlet and benefit can be gained even through the dry season. Not only that, others can benefit from the overflow of the reservoir. There will be availability when normal supplies are not there. They benefit from what the reservoir holds and others benefit from the overflow.

Only in the practice of allowing good things to flow through us do we see our God-given capacity for their stewardship. We begin to understand that there is great blessing in giving and being a channel. And only in surrendering that stewardship during the use of it do we experience the extent of the blessing God is desirous to put in to our reservoir. Often in God's way of doing things, the more we allow to flow over or through our reservoir, the more He brings in to keep it full, refreshing and useful.

Conclusion

Having a God-honoring reserve is predicated on two things. The first is that you enjoy it. God has given it to you as a wonderful blessing in your life. You daily need to be grateful for His goodness. The second is that you use it for Him. Wise stewardship of time, space, money, energy, opportunity, love, information and wisdom is an investment made in eternal things. It advances the kingdom of God and all the good and blessing that may imply for you and your family, church, community and world.

God is our ultimate reserve. We have everything in Christ. If our "assignment" from Him finds us feeling low on reserve, with the well appearing dry, God is there just as He is when we feel filled to the brim. Paul said he had learned a secret. It was good that others shared with him and strengthened him. Nevertheless, even without those resources he could still *do everything through Him who gave him strength." (Philippians 4:10–14)* God is our ultimate resource.

Coaching Moments

- Jesus said he came that you *"might have life to the full." (John 10:10)* What does that mean to you?
- In what areas do you already have a good reserve? How have you viewed that up until now? Is there any way in which your thinking needs to change?
- Do the reserves you have been blessed with have an outlet? Do God's fullness, grace and goodness flow through you to others—your spouse, family, missions, community etc.?
- Are there areas in your life where you feel particular stress that can be traced to not having enough reserve of something? Identify them.
- If you had more reserve in any one area, what would be different?
- How can you increase your capacity to hold what God may want you to have?

Coaching Challenges

- **CAPACITY:** Increase your capacity to hold what God may want to bring your way by the renewing of your mind. (Romans 12:2) Make a word study of that area of desired reserve in the Bible. For example, you may seek to have a reserve of peace and quietness in your life. Check out the word "peace" as it occurs throughout scripture. It will orient you to God's thoughts about it.

- **CLARITY:** Gain clarity about yourself and your situation. What attitudes, actions and beliefs have led you to where you are right now?
  - o Make a list of reserves that you have. Use the list at the beginning of the chapter or add to it. You may not have realized they were there before.
  - o Now make a list of reserves that are missing, for which you feel stress in your life. Having them in place would make a total difference.
- **COMMITMENT:** Action without a real commitment to follow through often fails. Commitment takes place in your head and your heart. This is where you develop a strategy to move forward.
  - o Create an action plan. It will either reduce your need for, or increase your supply of that desired reserve.
  - o Detail how you plan to increase your capacity to hold whatever it is, while you increase its presence in your life. Do you need to work on an attitude, gain some knowledge or change the way you approach things? Be specific.
  - o As you make a plan, go over it until you are satisfied that you can and will carry it out to completion. If a step causes you to hesitate, deal with it. Refine your plan and your commitment will grow.
- **COMPLETION:** This is the action step, doing what it takes to make it happen. Start. Pray. Trust God. Keep reviewing, refining and working your strategy to build the reserves into your life to which you feel God calling you.
  - o Put your action plan into effect. Remember to make it **SMART: S**pecific, **M**easurable, **A**chievable, **R**ealistic and having some **T**ime frame attached to it.
  - o Notice any barriers you encounter. Stop and deal with them. Don't let them stop you from your goal.

4 | EMBRACING THE WHOLE PERSON

By Terry L. Phillips

"I was introduced to you through the ICF coach refer-ral service and wondered if you can help me develop my management skills. I am the senior chemist in our company, and we are in the process of merging with another company. They also have a senior chemist. After the merger, only one of us will have a position. Managing others is the area in which I feel weakest. Also, since I am a foreigner and my English is not so good I feel I may not get the job. I am already giving consideration to migrat-ing to another country where I might have better opportunities."

That first e-mail from John was brief, to the point, pretty fo-cused; and yet I sensed an underlying tone of desperation. I was quite eager to get to know the person behind the comments. How-ever, as is often the case in coaching, we didn't meet face-to-face for months.

After the initial session and his completion of the Welcome Pack, required of all new coaching clients, I discovered that John is a Christian and quite involved in church activities. During the coach-ing sessions, I recognized that any time his comments referred to his faith his energy level would rise and his vocal tone actually changed. But reference to his work brought a lowered tone and sluggish response.

It didn't take many sessions to see the need to have John

focus on his WHOLE person, not just the work-related issues. As many people do, John seemed to leave a part of himself behind when he entered his workplace. His training as a chemist and his years of experience guided his hands, but he had left his "heart" outside. He lacked motivation, confidence and peace.

I asked him to give consideration to a metaphor that I first heard from Drs. Lee Smith and Janine Sandstrom from CoachWorks, an executive coaching company based in Dallas. Their presentation put handles on a concept that I had felt for years but could never verbalize adequately. My understanding of what they presented is this: in order to really have impact on a person's life, we must touch every part of his/her life. We must address intellectual, experiential and emotional needs.

Let's take a look at the WHOLE person.

The HEAD

All too often it seems that an inappropriate emphasis is placed on the "paper" qualifications the individual brings to the marketplace. The primary focus is on the person's Curricula Vitae or resumé. What an individual knows, or should know, by virtue of his/her educational background frequently seems to be the critical point in hiring a person for a job. This knowledge base is usually understood as the COGNITIVE INTELLIGENCE of the person.

On the other hand, some folks use the expression, "It's all in your HEAD," implying that certain things are a figment of one's imagination. My concern is when people say, "It's ALL in your head."

The HANDS

After a meticulous examination of the individual's C.V. or resumé, we look at his/her abilities. This includes a person's related work experience and skill base. Of course, this is an important consideration when seeking the appropriate person for a job. These abilities can be referred to as a person's BEHAVIORAL INTELLIGENCE. This would include what a person can "do." Some people so strongly identify with their job or what they do that their whole self-worth becomes a part of that picture. Helping those persons understand that this represents what they do, *not* who they are, is important.

The HEART

Today, we are finally beginning to recognize the value and importance of not only examining the "what" people do but also the "why." To truly understand a person's internal motivation we need to challenge them to examine their values, their feelings, and their relationships. Through the work of people like Howard Gardner and Daniel Goleman, we have come to a new awareness of what is referred to as EMOTIONAL INTELLIGENCE.

I find that people in career transition or, even more often, those facing what I call career crisis (dissatisfaction on the job) frequently show symptoms of a "heart" problem. More often than not, the etiology stems from values conflict. That conflict rises from differing values between the individual and the corporation.

John was suffering from what I identified as a heart problem. Looking to the merger of the two companies and having a new corporate culture thrust upon him caused a great deal of anxiety and fear.

I began to assist John in a personal examination of his values, relationships, and personal faith. I asked him how all of these fit into the corporate values of the new company and whether his relationships on the job brought life-giving energy to him or drained energy from him. Then we began to go through the Professional Foundations program from Corporate Coach U International.

After spending several weeks in personal assessment, John began to feel that his real need was to develop his inner spiritual man, not develop his management skills. But, he quickly began to see how the two were related.

He discovered that his true personal values and his motivation were based on a desire "to serve." This was especially clear as he examined his family life and his relationships within the church. He saw that his role was to help bring happiness and fulfillment to his wife, children, small group members, and other parishioners. In these arenas he felt secure and successful.

We then had a long discussion of Matthew 20:26-28: *"Whoever wants to become great among you must become your servant, and whoever wants to be first must be your slave – just as the Son of Man did not come to be served but to serve . . . ."*

I asked him to try to see himself as a Servant-Leader when he considered his role as a manager at work. Something happened in that moment. John saw himself as a WHOLE man. He was able to see how he could add value on the job by being his TRUE self. John was able to see the importance and necessity of embracing the WHOLE person.

Putting his life into proper perspective, he found that his personal calling could readily relate to his career and his abilities as well as his personal and church life. Clarity of perspective brought peace to John. But, more than that, it also brought confidence. Within a few months, he had brought the two work units together to function smoothly as one and eventually was asked to head the department.

He went from fear (ready to migrate) to confidence (position as senior chemist) to excellence (promoted to department head and hired a senior chemist to replace himself.)

God created us to function as a WHOLE person at ALL times. As believers we should have a clearer understanding of who we are and what we are about. We must not fall into the trap of the world by identifying ourselves only by what we do.

Ms. Tan's Story

Ms. Tan was brought into our lives by Divine Providence. She was the travel agent of choice for a friend who offered to purchase a ticket for my wife to travel with me for a training assignment in Taiwan.

On the same day our friend was giving the agent's name and number to my wife, I was teaching in a local Bible School. A student was assigned to share a brief devotional lesson and lead the class in prayer. She requested special prayer for a Ms. Tan. The student recently had opportunity to share her faith with this woman from another religious background. At that moment, I had not yet heard the name before; but something impressed me to open the class with an additional prayer for this individual.

Upon approval from the organization inviting me to Taiwan to bring my wife, I asked my wife for the contact number of the travel agent. What a coincidence! The name was the same as the person for whom we had prayed! I dialed the number and spoke to a very pleasant lady. I told her who I was, and she said that she was already holding the ticket for my wife. I then asked if she knew this young lady from the Bible College. Hearing her enthusiastic response caused me to make a very bold statement, "God must think you are a very special person."

After a long, pregnant pause, I heard the hesitant reply, "Why would you say that?" I then told her that I was present the previous day when a class of 60 people prayed for her – specifically. She exclaimed, "My God! (Later I was to learn that was her favorite expression.) I have those funny little bumps on my arm. Are you serious?"

That began an adventure with a person who truly sought God with her WHOLE person. Over the next year, she read books about Christianity, including the Bible, to increase her knowledge. She sought to "do" what she felt would bring her closer to God. She fasted, prayed, and attended Temple every morning for prayers. She even covertly attended Christian services whenever she could do so without creating problems with her family. We did not push her. We told her that the knowledge of God wasn't what she needed. We tried to explain that God wasn't impressed with our deeds. What He really wanted was a relationship that grew from our heart.

Her quest for that relationship brought a new zeal and enthusiasm to her work. She began to have a drive in her business other than just the "bottom line." The people around her began to see and experience something new as they related to her. She began to view the world through different eyes.

At one point, she enrolled for a class I taught at a local Bible School and actually made a personal commitment to Jesus. Unfortunately, my wife and I were her only support system. I had worked with her family business as a consultant and knew all the relatives, but they were not sympathetic to her changing religions.

My wife and I relocated to Hong Kong for six months to head a training program for missionaries. Upon our return, we discovered that our dear friend had replaced her quest for a relationship with God to an intellectual acceptance of Christianity. She had moved from the HEART to the HEAD. Today, we continue to pray for her Voyage of Discovery to carry her back to that personal relationship.

* * *

We have a powerful mandate from the Word. Paul has challenged us in Ephesians 4:22-24: "*. . . with regard to your former way of life, to put off your old self, which is being corrupted by its deceitful desires; to be made new in the attitude of your minds; and to put on the new self, created to be like God in true righteousness and holiness.*"

In many ways we can link this illustration of HEART, HEAD and HANDS to the truism: "You are a SPIRIT; you have a SOUL; you live in a BODY." Your spirit is your life from God, the *real you* on the inside. Your soul is your mind, your emotions and your will. It gives you your unique personality and character – who you are and whom you are becoming. All of this is carried in your earthly body with its five senses.

> *"May your WHOLE spirit, soul and body be kept blameless at the coming of our Lord Jesus Christ."*
> *1Thessalonians 5:23*

Coaching Moments

- When you go to the office or to the job, do you leave your HEART in San Francisco? (Or elsewhere?)
- What resources do you bring to your job in addition to your HEAD?
- Do you function in peace on the job?
- As you reread Paul's words in Ephesians 4, examine your *attitudes* on the job. Do they reflect the *new self* that Paul talks about?

Coaching Challenges

- Identify three values that give a sense of direction to your life.
- Try to describe in a single sentence your "reason for being."
- List ways you are using your HEAD and HANDS for the Kingdom of God.
- Discuss with your coach, husband, wife, significant other, or closest friend about ways you can bring a greater balance in your life by embracing the Whole Person.

5 | DEVELOPING GOD'S GIFTS

By Ruth Ledesma

"To one he gave five talents of money, to another two talents, and to another one talent, each according to his ability . . . ."
    Matthew 25:15

"There are different kinds of gifts, but the same Spirit. There are different kinds of service, but the same Lord. There are different kinds of working, but the same God works all of them in all men."
    1 Corinthians 12:4-6

"Every good and perfect gift is from above, coming down from the Father of the heavenly lights, who does not change like shifting shadows."
    1 James 1:17

"We have different gifts, according to the grace given us. If a man's gift is prophesying, let him use it in proportion to his faith. If it is serving, let him serve; if it is teaching, let him teach; if it is encouraging, let him encourage; if it is contributing to the needs of others, let him give generously; if it is leadership, let him govern diligently; if it is showing mercy, let him do it cheerfully."
    Romans 12:6-8

I often forget that the "talents" referred to in Matthew 25 are units of money. My forgetfulness is probably because I have generalized the concept across more than 25 years of counseling with people who have disabilities about career issues. I have come to believe we are called to rejoice in whatever gifts God has given and to make the best of them. If those gifts are in the form of money, as in the parable, then we are called to be good stewards of that money. When the gifts are less amenable to being a monetary measure of exchange, then perhaps we need to open our understanding further in order to appreciate fully the gifts with which God has blessed us. Coaching is one of the tools for opening our understanding.

Helen's Story

Helen had worked for 12 years as secretary to a successful realtor. She listened avidly as her boss described matching buyers and sellers and "just right" homes. She rejoiced when they found the best financing packages, especially the first-time homebuyers. On several occasions he had said, "Helen, you would be a terrific realtor. Why don't you take the training and give it a try?" But Helen always found a reason not to: "Oh, I couldn't possibly handle the negotiations," she would say. Or, "That kind of responsibility is not for me." She continued assisting her boss until she realized one day that she was being overwhelmed with sadness every day when she walked into her office. She consulted with her pastor who suggested she talk with a coach about career issues. She came to me very sure that she was not happy with her present work, but with not the faintest idea what to do about it.

We started by listing what Helen already knew. She certainly knew she no longer gained satisfaction from her work as a secretary. She also knew that the pay, although generous, left almost nothing when the family bills were paid. And she frequently worried about how she and her husband would manage when they retired. Helen also knew very clearly that she wanted God's will for her life but, like so many, couldn't figure out what that was in a very concrete, day-to-day way. She knew she was having difficulties making a connection between the agrarian images surrounding the topics of work in the Bible and her suburban life.

Our next task was to clarify what God's will meant to her in the abstract. As it happened, Helen was very clear that God wanted her to be productive in her work; but she had not realized that happiness and fulfillment were also part of the deal. Somewhere, she had picked up the idea that life on this earth is supposed to be, at least in part, a punishment, and that enduring the punishment stoically would bring her favor in God's eyes. Service too was supposed to be a sacrifice, not a joyful experience. Concordance studies brought to light several scriptures that she took as her own, especially *"Moreover, when God gives any man wealth and possessions, and enables him to enjoy them, to accept his lot and be happy in his work – this is a gift of God." (Ecclesiastes 5:19)* Helen was on her way to understanding that God wanted her work to be a source of productivity, happiness, fulfillment, and provision for herself and her family. And if serving didn't have to be sacrifice — well, that opened up all kinds of possibilities!

Then we got concrete about God's Will in Helen's life. We looked first at what the Bible says about who she is. One reference in particular spoke to her heart: *For you created my inmost being; you knit me together in my mother's womb. I praise you because I am fearfully and wonderfully made; your works are wonderful. I know that full well. (Psalm 139:13-14)* She came to understand, at least in theory, that she had a unique blend of gifts that God had chosen just for her. Yet when Helen listed her strengths and talents, it was a short list. Like so many capable people, she just assumed that everyone could do the things she found so easy. As we discussed the many tasks she routinely accomplished, she realized that she had been taking many of her talents for granted; and she became more grateful each day.

Along with the gratitude welling up inside her, she felt a growing sense of responsibility for her God-given talents. Further coaching helped Helen explore how she might leverage her talents and gifts to have the greatest impact. A real turning point came when she realized that she could serve God, herself, and other people much more effectively as a realtor than she could in a secretarial position. Her boss was overjoyed that she had finally "seen the light." He was eager to pay for Helen's training and licensing, so long as she promised to continue working as an associate realtor in his agency.

* * *

Professional athletes develop and hone their skills, making the most of their physical strength and agility. Gardeners nurture plants with their "green thumbs." Renowned writers polish their natural affinity for stringing words together in meaningful ways. To show their love, toddlers make the best Valentines in the world. Great composers and artists produce glorious music and visual images using the creativity with which they are endowed. Loving parents nourish their children's souls as well as their bodies when they teach and show them how to mold the best lives they can live.

The physical strength and agility, the 'green thumb, the affinity for words, the love, the creativity, the insight – they all come from God. Why does it happen that some of us welcome these gifts and make the most of them to benefit ourselves and the world around us, while others of us take these same kinds of gifts for granted or reject them outright as we strain and struggle to achieve goals built on our weaknesses? Why do some people see strengths and talents as wonderful gifts from God and others don't?

Andy's Story

Andy grew up convinced that he had to work hard to be a success. Easy subjects in school, like English and social studies, were left to take care of themselves while Andy put in long hours to make it in the more difficult math classes. Despite being an outstanding athlete, he had no interest in sports and focused single-mindedly on mastering math. Even when he was diagnosed with a learning disorder in math, he insisted that he was up to the challenge and remained in the regular math classes. Andy graduated from high school with honors and entered college, determined to become an accountant like his father. His advisor referred him to me for coaching when he "hit the wall" and could no longer manage the necessary grades in the math and accounting courses.

In coaching, Andy explored why he was convinced that he had to excel at the one thing he didn't do well. Obviously he was trying to please his father, so Andy agreed to list every way he could think of that he might please his father without engaging in math. He shared the list with his father who added quite a few more items to the list. Andy's father's love for him was totally unrelated to his ability to master math and accounting. Andy's father had no desire to push Andy to follow in his footsteps.

Still, Andy felt the overpowering need to focus on his only weakness; so we continued coaching around the options he had available now that he didn't have to be an accountant to please his father. I had a hunch that focusing on his math weakness might be a way to ignore what he really wanted to do with his life, so we started digging for the things that gave him joy and satisfaction. He developed a big case of "but-itis" as he revealed how much he enjoyed playing baseball, how he lost track of time when he was "messing about" with paints, and how much satisfaction he felt when he found just the right words to express a concept. To find out why he was rejecting these activities he so clearly enjoyed, I asked, "What would have to be true for you to be okay with doing one of these things as your profession?" He surprised himself and me when he blurted out "God would have to approve."

That was Andy's true turning point. We explored the source of the desires, pleasures, joys, and satisfaction he felt while engaging in these activities. We clarified his personal criteria for determining God's approval. Perhaps most significantly, we found the basis for his mistaken belief that "if an activity was easy and fun, the desire to engage in it must be from Satan" and Andy permanently laid it to rest. As a child, he had overheard some facetious comments and assumed they were true.

With his new understanding, Andy began exploring. He tried out and was picked for the university baseball team, despite his lack of team experience in high school. He decided to major in English and minor in art while determining exactly what he wanted to do.

Recognizing now that the desires of his heart come from God, Andy knows he has God's full approval to pursue a profession that he loves.

* * *

Regardless of what form they may take, the gifts and talents we receive from God are ours for using and developing to the fullest. If we turn our backs and refuse to acknowledge and nurture our gifts, for whatever misguided reasons, we reject the Giver as well as His gifts. Romans 12:6-8 lists only the smallest beginning of the multitude of ways God manifests His gifts to us in our lives. We are called to honor God with our grateful acceptance and use our precious gifts and talents to build happy and fulfilled lives that glorify God.

Coaching Moments

- For those who truly love God, all the strengths, gifts and talents come from God.
- You are responsible for what you do with God's gifts and talents.
- Recognize that you may have misunderstood God's will for you.
- The desires of your heart are from God.
- God will enable you to do His will. You don't have to struggle.
- God wants you to be happy in your life while glorifying Him.

Coaching Challenges

- Are you ready to test your understanding with a solid study of Biblical teaching?
- What is God's will for you? Describe it in the abstract and in specific detail.
- What are your strengths, gifts and talents? What is their source?
- How can you demonstrate your responsibility for these gifts and talents?
- Write out a detailed description of the career of your dreams.
- Compare your desired career and your understanding of God's will for you.
- What is still blocking you from having a career that is within God's will?
- How will you work with God to remove those blocks?

6 | ASSIGNMENTS AND RESTS

By Gary Wood

Stress-free living hardly seems possible. Who could be so naïve to think that you could go through life and not feel the stresses and strains of everyday living, not have to deal with the pressures of bills, traffic, family problems and intolerable people, not be faced with death, illness, loss and the pace of change. Add to that the tasks you take on out of spiritual and compassionate concern for those around you. How easy to conclude the stress-free life is a myth. Or is it?

Maybe we can't have the stress-less life, but we most surely can have the less stressed life. That is within reach. For the Christian, it is built on two practical building blocks – assignments and rests. Both are part of God's plan. We work or carry something for Him, and then we rest. We overstep the principle only to experience overload and dissatisfaction or to cause it for others.

Assignments

As young people, we spend considerable time wondering what it is that the Lord wants us to do. What career do I pursue? Should I consider longer-term mission work? We talk, seek counsel, explore, and pray about it. Finally, we make a decision and move ahead with studies. We conclude that we are where God wants us to be. (Acts 27:23, 2 Timothy 1:3) That is the definition of an assignment. We are where God wants us to be and doing what we feel He wants us to be doing. The definition applies equally to a small project or an entire career.

Assignments have beginnings and endings. We agree to take a task on, and we finish it. (John 17:4) We are employed one place, and we change employers. We serve a certain function at church for a time and then feel a timely readiness for others to take over. These are all physical assignments. But there are other assignments as well, such as illness or sharing a burden with someone else. (2 Corinthians 1:5-9) These are the types of things we go through or feel more than being things we set out to do. In all of this, there is a rhythm, a flow that starts when we are young and progresses right through old age. If we viewed what we do as assignments from God, with beginnings and endings, we would be much more conscious of the times in between, which have been designed for our renewal. Both are placed before us as part of a divine plan.

Rests

Rest is a natural starting point. Farmers understand the value of letting land lie unused for a season. It is called lying fallow. The ground has a chance to be without the stress of supplying for demanding crops that have been planted. Neglect this principle of lying fallow, and sustained crops can only grow by constant addition of fertilizer to replace the deficiencies in the soil.

Once my wife and I drove by hundreds of acres of lush, productive, garden cropland. The earth was dark, and we remarked how much we would like a few truckloads dumped in our garden. Then someone informed me that the earth was actually dead. It had basically lost its ability to perform. Its only function now was as a medium to contain the plants. It was the heavy fertilizing that really fed the growth.

The experience of far too many people is similar to that land. While others applaud the good results and the crop looks great, the worker is left feeling barren from having done too much for too long without stopping to renew. Fallowness is vital to regain a sense of peace, balance, and renewed focus outside of the hectic rush to meet the needs of people and tasks. (Mark 6:30-32)

More than You Were Assigned

You feel confident that the work you are considering doing, whether in the church or in the world are what the Lord has asked you to do. In response, you commit yourself to carry out this assignment uniquely given to you. (Colossians 4:17) After some time, one of two things happens. In the course of doing the work, you see other things that could be done; so you initiate them too. Or, in the course of the work, others want to add more programs and responsibilities. You know that the work takes time and energy, but you agree to it. Without additional structure and support, the level of stress may begin to rise.

Did God call you to this? Not necessarily. You saw new things to do, or others asked you to do additional tasks. (Romans 12:3-8) Here's the point. In cases where overload and burnout occur, quite possibly we have overstepped the original assignment, which God gave us to do in the natural course of living. Of course, when we see good results, we conclude that the end justifies the means and that it must have been our job to do. However, there is a cost. Often stress escalates to overload which, unchecked, leads to burnout.

Steve's Experience

Steve is a consultant who feels thankful for all of the client work that comes his way. He has a respected consulting practice, maintaining a balance between family and work. A couple of years ago, Steve and his wife decided to purchase a very large home. The home was more than they ever anticipated needing. Comparing prices in this range of upscale homes, they reasoned it was a bargain they couldn't pass up and the financial stretch would be worth it.

Ultimately the burden of this decision began showing itself. Unanticipated expenses associated with the home meant that Steve had to push the limits at work. Steve experienced long hours, increasingly rushed time on-site with clients and less time at home. The results were an intact-but-strained relationship with his wife, client complaints, failing accounts, and increasing frustration for Steve.

Scripture reveals God's pattern. It is work, rest, work, and rest. God Himself worked six days and rested on the seventh. (Genesis. 2:2,3) This is the divine pattern for us to follow. Is it as simple as saying we should not work on Sunday? No. That may be the case, but it is not the point. The point is that after work there is rest, and before work there is rest. We feel led by God to our vocation or project. It may last days, weeks or months, but it will be finished. Then we are in a rest period before God gives us another assignment.

On another level we may feel led to other long-term patterns, such as buying a home in a particular area. A move like this may last many years, but it too can be considered an assignment.

Steve broke the pattern of rest, work and rest. His pattern became work, work and work. He could trace the beginning of this slide back to the decision to buy the house. The support of the coaching relationship helped Steve to see clearly the whole story. He was asked to make a list of those things in life he felt confident were clearly "assigned" by God and those that were not. Then he was asked to check off what was still ongoing and what was completed. Once he stated it clearly, Steve could see there was no indication that the assignment of their original home was over. In fact it had been in a neighborhood they felt led to move into.

Steve wrote down the steps that led him to where he was. Discussing it with his wife, they realized that his career had been in balance and going well prior to this buying decision. Steve stopped pointing blame elsewhere and took responsibility for his situation. Because of newfound clarity, he and his wife together could take steps to correct their situation. They put the house on the market within two weeks. Steve revisited his consulting practice and wrote out who his ideal clients were and what his ideal practice would look like in the future.

He began to set some limits on his time away from home. And he began concluding existing contracts with a positive attitude that reflected the future they were attracting. The home sold in reasonable time and they moved into a lovely, and easily affordable home where they knew all costs and saw a good future for their growing family.

Steve looks back now and sees that there were times God was providing for rest; but he and his wife didn't catch on, missed it, and suffered the consequent stress. Their situation was not apparent to most people. They just kept doing what they had been doing, struggling to be efficient and outwardly cheerful. But, his clients picked up Steve's reality as their dissatisfaction with his work grew. Privately, the toll of stress kept mounting until he got the lesson and took action on it. Steve can now enjoy a rest. His life has stabilized, giving him balance and satisfaction once again.

Steve took the steps to restore balance in his life. Not knowing where the search would lead, he retained a coach to provide structure and support. He chose a coach who could assist him to achieve some harmony between his faith and his activities. This investment reaped rewards for Steve and his family and continues to do so.

Coaching Moments

- How long can you keep working at one thing without a break? What effect does that have on you? Physically? Emotionally? Socially?
- What is the difference between a single project and a long-term commitment?
- If you had to take a furlough from one responsibility, what

would it be? What would you gain or lose by stepping back? What do you feel God might be leading you to do?
· What are some of the assignments God has given you throughout your Christian experience?
· Is there any indication that one of your assignments may be drawing to a close?

Coaching Challenges

· Write down exactly the assignment God is asking of you. Always be clear about this.
· Assume that many assignments will grow. Leave room for this to happen, but control it. Don't let it control you.
· Put suitable structures and support in place. Attend to such things as financial, administrative, or personal support. Retain the services of a coach if this will serve you.
· Calculate the cost. Are you prepared to take this on? Make sure you know what this will mean to your family, finances, social life and to you personally. What if the commitment required were to double? Could you handle it?
· Be clear at the beginning. Cover all the details you can possibly think of before you start. Be clear with others about what you can and cannot do, what you feel capable of taking on, and what you don't. Write it down so everybody is clear. Don't add complexities that are not needed. Finish the specific task you have agreed to. (2 Timothy 4:7) Once in progress or done, consider any additions carefully.

7 | DRAWING YOUR LINE IN THE SAND:

When you want to say "no", but "yes" comes out of your mouth

By Judy McMaster Santos

The buzz about the importance of setting boundaries is a valid one. When you set a personal boundary, you symbolically draw a line in the sand and let people know that they may not intrude into your personal space by crossing that line. It is a result of deliberately deciding what is going to be okay with you, sticking with your decision and applying consequences, if necessary. Often, setting boundaries is a way of validating yourself and commanding respect from others. There is nothing mean spirited about this. Having good boundaries allows you to maintain control of what and whom you allow into your life in order to reach your own highest potential while honoring your values. It is often said that when you say "no" to someone, you are saying "yes" to yourself. On the surface, that seems like a very humanistic approach, and it certainly can be. However if you know yourself to be a child of God, setting good boundaries is a way of preventing distractions that can divert you from the path that you and the Lord embark upon daily. Putting responsible boundaries in place is a form of self-care and a demonstration of self-respect. We are instructed through the Word in many places to rest and restore ourselves from our work and pay attention to what makes us whole.

" ... *And God blessed the seventh day and made it holy, because on it he rested from all the work of creating that he had done.*"
Genesis 2:2

"*Be still before the Lord.*"
Psalm 37:7

"*Be still and know that I am God.*"
Psalm 46:10

"*... Jesus ... went off to a solitary place, where he prayed.*"
Mark 1:35

"*But Jesus often withdrew to lonely places and prayed.*"
Luke 5:16

"*I have not come to call the righteous, but sinners to repentance.*"
Luke 5:32

"*(God) He restores my soul.*"
Psalm 23:3

"*... Jesus went out into the hills to pray, and spent the night praying to God.*"
Luke 6:12

Everybody has some boundaries, or personal rules, already in place. For example, you may not wish to discuss your personal finances with anyone. Therefore you stop the questions, either by ignoring them, or simply saying "I only discuss my finances with my CPA and my financial planner." An explanation is not necessary.

You may decide that you will no longer be on the receiving side of negative name-calling. You may have to say that you do not stay in the presence of someone who is name-calling and that, if it continues, you will remove yourself from that situation. Then, you must follow through.

As a parent you may have some rules for your children. For example, they don't enter the bedroom if the door is closed, or no kitchen equipment leaves the kitchen. While these decisions may be identified in your mind as common sense rules, rather than boundaries, they speak of your need to have your personal space or that your property be respected.

When it comes to drawing those lines in the sand with other adults however, we are not necessarily in a position of authority, and we all too often turn into marshmallows. The problems usually arise when you are asked to stretch in areas that are normally part of your life.

Some people, either by personality or conditioning, are very naturally clear about their boundaries and accustomed to going through life without having those questioned.

For others, saying "no" can be tough. The challenge exists for those raised in an environment where the word "should" was often used, and the word "choose" was not!

Christians who are committed to serving the Lord and being obedient to the leading of the Holy Spirit often feel internal conflict when they are asked to do something "for Him". We want to do the right thing and we don't want to be unkind or insensitive to other people. However, there is a fine line between being a victim of manipulation and being obedient to the Lord. Prayer becomes the important factor here. When we invite the Lord into our day and our decisions, He guides us in making the right choices. While sometimes we wish there would be a billboard to give us clear direction, we do have a way of knowing that comes from being sensitive to His leading.

An unspoken fact in this society is that good-hearted people don't say "no" when they are asked to do something. They help. They make personal sacrifices for the good of the cause. They use their God-given talents. They have a servant's heart and cheerfully share with others. They don't seem to mind the company of the people whom others avoid. At all costs, they put the needs of others before their own, and do it without complaint. They always manage to be available, whenever needed. They don't get upset if people treat them badly, they just keep giving and hope to be salt and light in a hurting world.

At the very least, this sounds noble. Scripture seems to substantiate this, starting with the Golden Rule. *"Do unto others as you would have them do unto you." "Love your neighbor as yourself." (Luke 10:27)*

A sacrificial life is praised by others. People are often told that they are earning jewels for their crown. They earn a reputation, based on acts of love and kindness. They are the people who always manage to squeeze in one more project, help one more person, or chair one more committee.

Sometimes however, being known as a capable, generous person with a willingness to help creates a difficult situation. Without good boundaries, others may use the name of God in order to manipulate you into saying "yes." The problem is, of course, that saying "yes" to everybody and everything strips you of your reserves and wears you out. And when you are in that condition, you can't function effectively for the Lord, for yourself or for others.

The question becomes, who do you have to BE and what has to be in place so that you can fulfill the commission of Jesus to love and to serve?

What is necessary in your life, so that you are spiritually, physically, mentally, emotionally and even financially available to help others? This is a question very often overlooked by believers and one that surfaces often in coaching.

Karen's Story

Consider my client, Karen. As a busy wife and mom she chose not to work outside their home while raising their children. She was involved in leading the women's ministry at church, and she also sang in the choir. Life was hectic, but she managed to juggle complex schedules and keep the household humming like a well-oiled machine. As planned, Karen re-entered the outside work force in order to help financially when their first-born entered college. She landed a job in a lovely office that was close to home.

With diligence and planning that was so much a part of Karen's style, she resigned from the women's ministry, because they met during the day when she would be working. Shortly before Karen went back to work, she held a family meeting and explained that she would be available 50 hours less each week. She set up a new routine for the family, which included additional responsibilities for their teenagers. She carefully explained that she was continuing to help the family, but in a different way, so that a college education could be a reality for all. She asked for their cooperation. Everyone seemed to understand and nodded in agreement.

Karen began coaching one month after she went back to work. She felt like she was in overload. She enjoyed her job but found it to be more exhausting than she anticipated.

"I get home from work and all I want to do is take a nap! The first week it was great!

"The kids all followed through with their responsibilities, dinner was on the table at 6 p.m. and the kitchen was cleaned up by 8:00. But since then, it's been a downhill spiral. I wind up making dinner because everybody is hungry. The kids seem to have a dozen reasons why they can't be home in time to get things done. My son keeps forgetting to pick up my daughter from basketball practice, and there are piles of unfolded laundry all over the house. They just don't get it!

"And, I've had five or six calls from people at church, because the women's ministry is in trouble. They don't have any strong leadership to take over my position and they keep asking me to help out. I feel so guilty. I have trouble saying 'no' when people ask me to help. When I do, I always feel like I have to provide a long explanation. It's not that I think I am indispensable, it just seems like I would be letting people down. Now I don't know what to do! It feels like I had just added a complication to my life by working, and instead of replacing what I was doing before, I just added more to it."

We worked on identifying her most important values. She had a long list but finally managed to prioritize them. At the top of her list was doing what God wants her to do. As she began to look at the people and the responsibilities in her life, she was able to see not only her roles, but also what she needed to do in order to keep her behavior in line with her values.

As she looked at the frustrations that occurred since going back to work, what became clear to her was that her teenagers were, perhaps without intent, testing out Mom. Once Karen recognized that, she found the home situation was pretty easy to solve. She called a second family meeting to underline the reality of the new structure. This time, though, she followed through, without allowing guilt to reign, insisting that others fulfill their responsibilities. Because she was able to do this without expressing disappointment or anger, her requests were accepted.

As Karen looked at the requests and pleas to get involved once again at some level in the women's ministry at church, she was able to see that people were looking to her instead of to God. She knew there were capable women in the group who were able to lead. Karen struggled with her guilty feelings about saying "no" to holding evening or Saturday meetings and getting involved in the issues the new leadership was facing. Meanwhile, the group was accepting the fact she was no longer available and prayerfully getting the problems solved and the group back on its feet. Only when Karen was able to be firm and let go were others clear that they had to look to the Lord to provide His solution.

Coaching Moments

- How would you have to see yourself differently in order to be a person respected by others?
- What would have to change so you could give yourself permission to establish your boundaries?
- Do you feel guilty when you say 'no' and obliged to offer an explanation?
- Do you find yourself in conflict when you are asked to do something you don't want to do?
- Who in your life does not respect you?

Coaching Challenges

- Write down the names of the people who are closest to you. Write a sentence or two to describe the relationship.
- Make a list of the requirements you have for people to be close to you. How important is it that these people share your faith? Acknowledge your feelings? Forgive easily? Respect your values?
- Write down the names of people who tend to cause you internal conflict. What are they asking of you that makes you uncomfortable? How does their presence affect you?
- Establish a plan of action to deal with the people and situations in the item above.
- Practice aloud (with your coach or a friend) what needs to be said in a neutral tone of voice.

8 | CHOICES

By Carwin Dover

God gives us the option of making choices. So how do you maximize this gift to your benefit and to God's glory, rather than being caught up in the "shoulds" and "gottas" and . . .?

The classic question you will probably hear frequently from your Christian coach is, "What do you want?"

When I first began to check out the profession of coaching, I thought, "Here we go! This is just another secular approach to nurture selfishness."

Interestingly enough, within a few days of having that thought, my pastor caught my ear as he was reading scripture from the gospels. I must admit, I didn't think I was paying much attention, but my mental wanderings suddenly became very focused! "What do you want?" was all I heard.

"Who said that? Where does it say that in the Bible?" My indignation and false Christian pride were spurring me on to find out what my pastor could possibly be teaching today!

The verse that caught my ear is from Matthew 20: 29-34. Jesus asked two blind me who were calling for him as his walked down a road, "What do you want me to do for you?" Their choice was to receive their sight. They were granted their request. They went with Jesus as he continued his walk.

Do you notice anything interesting about Jesus' question? What about His answer? It doesn't appear that Jesus responded with, "You know you really *should* ask for your sins to be forgiven." As you review the conversations Jesus had with people, notice how He cut out the *shoulds* and skipped to the bottom line. "Do it!" No "shoulds" or "oughts", just do it. "Go and sin no more." "Feed my sheep." "Be kind." "Love your neighbor."

Here is another observation. Notice that Jesus does not give specific directions. He allows and encourages choices. Just think for a moment of all the choices available to respond to "Feed my sheep" or "Love your neighbor."

Choices abound! Not only do you have choices when answering the question, "What do you want?" but you have choices for "What will be your response when you receive what you want?" Remember, receiving opens up many choices for response.

What Do You Want?

If Jesus passed by and asked you, "What do you want me to do for you?" what do you hope you would say? The choices are many. Which would you name first?

· What you want to have?
· What you want to do?
· What you want to be?

The blind men wanted to have healing. They received it. What other choices did they have? Could they have maximized their gift from Jesus with a different request? Could they maximize their gift of healing after they received it?

Take a moment as you ponder the question, "What do you want me to do for you?" Begin to answer the above three questions.

What other choices did the blind men have?

When you go into a restaurant, the waiter will give you a menu. You may decide to have a steak, but what other choices do you have? When Jesus asked the blind men, "What do you want me to do for you?" what are 10 other choices they could have made?

Look at your list of 10 choices. Are any of the choices you suggest bad or immoral choices? Probably not. Do you think Jesus would have honored any other choices by the blind men had they not asked for healing?

Could the blind men have maximized their position with a different request?

Suppose the blind men made a different request. For instance, the blind men probably knew someone who was worse off than they were. Would their position with Jesus or with the crowds or with themselves have been better if they said, "I know this widow who is starving to death because she is sick and can't get to the market. Would you please heal her?"

It is impossible to answer such a question. It is an important question to ask yourself, however. Am I settling for a request or goal that is only temporary and short term? Is there a better response to "What do you want from me?"

Take the time to know what you want. An impulsive answer may not give you what you really want. The blind men were very sure of what they wanted. There was probably not a day that passed but what they didn't renew their desire to see. They knew what they wanted and did not allow any possible distractions to rise to the top of their priorities when Jesus asked the question of a lifetime. It seems obvious, but without a definite sense of direction, an impulsive urge has the power to take you down unfruitful paths.

What Will Be Your Response When You Receive What You Want?

The blind men were thankful. And what did they do in response? They followed Jesus. Where did that take them? Think of all the ways they might have responded to their new sight. Make a list of 101 things you think you might do with new sight.

When you receive what you want, you will respond. Take the time to plan some responses to your newfound sight. The character inside you will have a great deal to do with your response. What are you doing to develop the foundation of your response?

Do you suppose the suffering and sacrifices over the years by the blind men had anything to do with building their character? What made it possible for them to respond by following Jesus after their healing? Healing in and of itself does not guarantee thankfulness. Remember, we have choices! Do you recall the story of the 10 people with leprosy who were healed by Jesus? They all took off for town. Only one stopped, turned around and went back to thank Jesus.

When you plan for a response to receiving what you want, you are reinforcing your faith and belief that it will happen. Plan well.

Words of Encouragement!

Are you ready for some Good News? God's Grace is dynamic and constantly growing. You do not have to "be right" when you answer the question, "What do you want?" You do not even have to respond "the right way" when you receive what you want. As long as there is Grace, you can keep at it and respond to God's gentle nudging.

It is my suspicion that the blind men grew spiritually even though their request was just for physical healing. That seems to be the way Jesus operated. He took care of spiritual healing and growth in addition to healing and feeding the crowds.

As you make a choice and work towards it, stay alert. Many gifts will come your way. Sometimes the gifts will change your original direction. Sometimes the gifts will surpass your wildest dreams. The fascinating thing that happens is that as you move toward the choices you want, God has a way of offering guidance.

Those questions are inspired by God. It is not that a Christian coach has an inside track to God. It is, rather, that a Christian coach is more likely to be in tune with God due to his/her own personal relationship with Jesus.

Just think of the possible results of two people who are actively relating to God when they begin to act on some of the choices presented to them.

One of the valuable exercises a Christian coach will usually provide is the question, "What do you want?" Whether you say it or your coach says it, begin to answer the question as though Jesus were asking you personally, "What do you want me to do for you?"

As you begin, accept your first answers if they are such things as "More money, more time, a new car, a new house and a vacation around the world." Yet keep writing. Assume you now have more money, time and things. What do you imagine you will want now?

Your Christian coach will probably encourage you to continue your list to include what you want to be. Your list will begin to take on a different perspective. Such things as, "be generous, be kind, be loving and be faithful" will start to appear on your wish list. That's when you will begin to become aware of the depth of the question, "What do you want me to do for you?"

Take your list even further. Go back to the beginning of your list with the assumption you asked Jesus something from your "I want to be" section. For instance, if you said to Jesus, "I want you to give me a spirit of generosity" assume Jesus gave it to you. What is happening to your vision now? What is the healing you are now beginning to experience? I wonder if the blind men experienced such healing when they received new vision? Do you suppose their spirit also received vision as well as their eyes?

Coaching Moments

- During your quiet time, will you take time to ask for what you want and ask God to help make your requests of Him to be in line with His requests of you?
- Will you take time to share your answers to the question, "What do you want me to do for you?" Include such people as your spouse, children, and close friend.
- As you review your list of wants and prioritize it, what consistently remains in the top five positions? What are you doing to make it possible to receive what you want?
- What will it be like when you have received what you want?
- What do you plan to do after you have received what you want?
- What other choices do you have if a roadblock guides you in another direction? What are 10 other choices you have for each of the top five priorities you have?

Coaching Challenges

- Answer the following questions for each of the Top 10 priorities on your "What do you want?" list:
  - o What helped you decide the number for each priority?
  - o Why do you think Jesus would want to grant your request?
  - o What will you do when you receive each request?
  - o What are three variations Jesus might give for each Top 10?
- List 10 choices you have in the process of receiving what you want. Which of the choices will help you the most? Which choices may sabotage your efforts?
- List 10 choices Jesus has in granting your wish for each of your Top 10 priorities. (Do you remember the story of the

man who asked God to rescue him from floods surrounding his home? He refused the canoe, the powerboat and the helicopter. Later in heaven, God asked him why he refused them. The man replied, "I was waiting for you to rescue me!")

- Take each of your Top 10 priorities and write your observations of how Jesus has already begun to grant your request. Now make a list of ways in which you have responded positively to His gifts. Also make a list of ways in which you have missed, ignored or refused His gifts. What can you begin to do to be aware of Jesus' responses to your requests? What can you do to be thankful when you receive one of your choices? What can you do when you are not particularly thankful for the gift, but know it is a gift from God?

- The process of developing your choices is unending. As you receive some of your choices, new ones will come along. What are five ways you can be intentional about reviewing and renewing your choices?

9 | COMPLETION:

Putting the Past Behind

By Timothy E. Ursiny, Ph.D.

"Therefore, if you are offering your gift at the altar and there remember that your brother has something against you, leave your gift there in front of the altar. First go and be reconciled with your brother; then come and offer your gift."
Matthew 5:23-24

So you are heading to Church; and you are ready to belt out those hymns, take notes during the sermon, contribute financially to the work of the Church, and focus on the glory of our Lord while you bring great praise to Him. What could possibly be more important than offering your praise and your gifts to the Lord? Surely, this is your priority as a Christian, to glorify our Creator. Yet, Matthew clearly instructs in the passage above that if you have conflict with anyone, resolving the conflict takes priority before going to "the altar". While this passage of the Bible mainly refers to how to deal with anger and conflict among believers I believe that it also illustrates a powerful concept found in coaching: putting the past behind.

Read that paragraph again. Why did Matthew (as guided by the Holy Spirit) feel that resolving an issue with another human being was so important that it needed to be dealt with before honoring God at the altar? Perhaps, it is because we cannot *fully* honor our Lord unless we have dealt with the messes that we have created in our lives. Perhaps there is something that holds us back from our full expression of praise when our past has not been resolved. Think about it. How can you fully honor the God of second chances, love, and forgiveness, the God who resolved our sins through the death of His son, if you fail to address the issue of those you have injured or even, those who have injured you?

Coaching takes this concept of putting the past behind and addresses how unresolved issues from the past can limit us in our daily living as well as in our relationship with God. We can look at many examples of unresolved issues. Some possibilities are:

- Trauma from childhood
- Neglect from childhood
- Shame over previous actions before becoming a Christian
- Shame over previous actions after becoming a Christian
- Doing a less-than-adequate job on a task that returns to haunt you
- Guilt over the lack of some action on your part (like regular devotions or prayer)
- Resentment toward someone who has hurt you in the past

When any of the unresolved issues above continue to haunt our thoughts or impact our behavior we need to find ways to free ourselves of their distracting influence.

Before becoming a coach, I worked as a clinical psychologist for seven years. In that time, I met many people who were held in bondage by the past. For some, it was the personal shame of something that they had done wrong. For others, it was the recurring mental anguish as they re-experienced memories of pain that someone else had put them through. Other types of individuals were sitting in my office because someone made them come see me (usually a spouse who was at the end of her/his rope). These individuals never thought of the past and found it ridiculous that they had to come see a psychologist. Often these reluctant clients were causing pain to others because they were failing to face some events or patterns from their past that were still affecting them. Sometimes it was something that they did, and sometimes it was something that someone else did to them.

We can conceptualize these individuals in four categories as represented in Figure 9-1.

	When you are wrong	When someone has wronged you
Often re-experiences the past	Shame Stuck	Victim Stuck
Refuses to deal with the past	Hard Hearted	Repressed

Figure 9-1: Ways of dealing with the past

Those who were re-experiencing their painful memories would come to my office looking for peace. They wanted to alleviate the pain that they were experiencing in their lives and learn to live the "abundant life" that other Christians seemed to be living. Those who were being coerced to visit a "shrink" just wanted to do whatever they needed to do to get out of the experience (although many, in time, found great value from dealing with their issues).

As a coach, I have had similar experiences, but at a less intense level. Many individuals enter a coaching relationship because they are not completely happy with the direction of their lives. Some individuals are fairly content but experience a nagging feeling that there is something more "out there."

In coaching, we focus on our future selves – the person we are trying to be. There is far less focus on the past and much greater talk of growth, challenge, and progress. Therefore, when someone starts a coaching relationship, it is important that they do not have excess baggage from the past that will interfere or slow down their progress.

Mac's Story

Mac is an example of a *shame stuck* individual who entered coaching because he wanted more balance in his life. Mac had been what most people would call a workaholic for most of his life. He had known a colleague who had gone through coaching and who seemed to be at more peace in his life. This intrigued Mac enough to call me. I gave Mac a Life Balance Assessment to complete at our first session. He was very content in many areas of his life until he came to the family category. With just a little questioning, Mac started forming tears in his eyes. As he embarrassingly wiped a tear off his cheek, he talked of his relationship to his children.

Although he loved the Lord and was a committed Christian, Mac had made some (in his words), terrible mistakes as a father. His children were all grown and living away from home. They rarely visited and seemed very caught up in their own careers and families. Mac never knew that it was important to tell his kids that he loved them. He had been a great provider, financially, for the family; but he never knew how to care emotionally. He was a proud man and was not used to talking about his feelings. He had thought many times of talking with them about how he failed as a father but was too embarrassed and humiliated to do so. However, he soon came to realize that he needed to deal with this issue in order to live more abundantly.

Through a series of coaching sessions, Mac decided that it was time to deal with his former actions as a father. Mac wrote letters to each of his children apologizing for his distance over the years. He arranged times to meet with them individually to give them a chance to express their feelings about the past and come to some resolution together. Over the course of several months he developed closer relationships with his children and felt great relief. He and his children forgave him for the past.

Mac was now ready to focus on his present life, which included being a father of excellence.

So, how do you distance yourself from the past? Here are the main steps that I and other coaches have found necessary to take in order to let go of the past.

- Be able to look the past in the eye and fully understand it. You can't deal with something that you refuse to look at or comprehend.
- Believe that you can have freedom from the past. You don't have to be a victim of what has happened to you or a victim of shame all of your life because of something you have done.
- Embrace the full grace given to you through the love of Christ. As a Christian, you talk of grace; but do you really understand it? If you repent from your past, then God has forgiven you. Not to accept this is to slap the face of our Savior.
- Talk about each issue with someone you trust. There is something very cleansing about sharing your struggles with others. God indeed built us for community.
- Take any actions necessary to resolve the issue. The actions may not be easy, but you will feel better if you do them.
- Do everything today with integrity and excellence so that you can look back over your life with satisfaction rather than pain or shame.
- Forgive anyone who has hurt you and is repentant of his or her actions.
- Live a life of obedience to Christ so that shame does not grab you again. If you are a Christian, you will feel guilt until you obey. To continue to sin and rely on God's forgiveness is an abuse of the grace you are given. Repentance means to turn away from the old behavior.

· Seek therapy from a Christian counselor if you are unable to free yourself from the past through coaching, pastoral guidance, or help from your community.

Conclusion

To break free of the bondage of the past is consistent with breaking free of the bondage of sin. We become new people. God tosses our sinful past into the deepest of oceans. Let's leave it there and go on to be people of love, joy, and integrity.

Coaching Moments

· What important life events have shaped you both positively and negatively?
· What memories from the past keep distracting you from living at your fullest?
· What have you done in the past that still evokes feelings of guilt or shame?
· How well are you living a life of excellence that will prevent unresolved issues from developing for the future?
· Which describes your connection to the past best? Shame stuck? Victim Stuck? Hard Hearted? Repressed? Free?

Coaching Challenges

	Pain (How does this hurt you?)	Pleasure (How does this help you?)
Often re-experiencing the past		
Refusing to deal with the past		
Dealing with the past adequately and then living life abundantly		

Figure 9-2: Pain/pleasure chart

- Use the pain/pleasure chart in Figure 9-2 to help you fully understand the grip that the past has on you. Keep it where you will be reminded to read it everyday to motivate you to let go of the past.
- Write a letter to someone who has hurt you in the past. This letter is just for you and is not to be mailed. Be completely free in your expressions of feelings.
- Write a letter to God about your past. Ask for help in the areas where you need it the most.
- If you have an issue that is unresolved with someone, go deal with it. Remember, "Leave your offering on the altar". If you need help from a third party to bring peace, then ask for it.
- Keep a "Feelings Journal" to see if any issues that represent themes from the past keep coming up in your life. Form a strategy for dealing with these. One way to journal this is to keep track of what events cause what feelings. Then look at what you are saying to yourself about the event. Are your self-statements true? Is thinking that way helpful? If not, work at saying the truth to yourself.

10 | ACCEPTANCE

By Marilyn O'Hearne

What is acceptance, and what does it mean to us as Christians? The dictionary definition is "favorable reception, approval." What does our culture approve, and which types of people do we approve most frequently?

In the United States now, what we value and therefore approve and receive favorably are youth, beauty, career achievements, busy-ness, material wealth and what it can buy: nice clothes, car, home, education. What do these have in common? They are external ways we judge a person by looking at their body, their belongings, and their schedule.

"I am part of the 10 percent of US women who are content with their bodies," I say, thinking I am exaggerating. I'm not perfect, mind you. You can enjoy high self-esteem with a good body image, no matter what the shape of the body. Then I read that 70 percent of US women believe they are overweight. Fifty-eight percent of normal-weight women and 29 percent of normal-weight men share that perception. In a study of 10-year-old girls, 31 percent "felt fat." This preoccupation with thinness and comparing ourselves, especially women, to a non-realistic ideal like Barbie dolls and cover girls is literally killing us (the end result of eating disorders). The media acts as a powerful reinforcer of this external emphasis. Our culture's self focus also contributes to the importance placed on making a favorable impression rather than integrity.

Men, on the other hand, have been socialized to focus on their achievements and may define themselves as their work. This results in the health risk of an earlier death, usually from a heart attack. (Women outlive their husbands by an average of seven years.) As the pendulum has swung back to women having their own careers, they now are at higher risk for heart attacks as well. You are not your work! You are you.

Under what conditions does God approve of us? Is it based on externals? No, it is focused on who we are on the inside. God goes beyond approval to love us unconditionally based on our birthright and our response to Him. As coaches, we model and practice this non-judgmental, unconditional acceptance with our clients. Knowing that we are loved, accepted, and that life has meaning and purpose results in inner peace and high self-esteem. "What you are is God's gift to you. What you make of yourself is your gift to God," goes the saying.

"Then God said, 'Let us make man in our image . . . So God created man in his image, in the image of God he created him; male and female he created them.'" (Genesis 1:26, 27) According to our birthright, we are made in the image of God. One of the definitions of image is "to mirror or reflect." So we are made to mirror or reflect God and his unconditional love and acceptance of ourselves and others. *"A new commandment I give to you, that you love one another; even as I have loved you, that you also love one another."* (John 13:34)

Is this based on externals? No. Instead of looking in a glass mirror at our physical reflection for a clear image of ourselves, we can look in the mirror of God's Word. As coaches, we serve as our client's mirror, reflecting back what is said and unsaid. We listen through the Holy Spirit for words not spoken.

During one of my talks, a woman said, "It sounds like as a coach you partner with clients to help them reach the top of the Maslow hierarchy, self-actualization." Maslow's theory is that we are driven to achieve this higher order of existence, where we have a high acceptance of self and others, with little need to be judgmental or rejecting. God can use Christian coaches to facilitate reaching this level of acceptance.

Accepting means more than simply acknowledging or admitting. We contemplate, absorb, experience, and stand in the presence of God's acceptance. Like the Velveteen Rabbit, we are real when we have been loved so much that a little of our outer selves has rubbed off, showing our imperfection. We can accept ourselves and others without having "made it" yet, without liking or condoning, just as we can forgive without condoning. We can accept what is and be determined to grow and develop from there. Love who you are right now: the person you're becoming. Be patient with yourself. Set realistic expectations, rather than comparing yourself to an ideal. We can strive for excellence without making this the basis of our self-judgment.

What natural tendencies do we want to avoid in order to experience God's acceptance?

· Comparing ourselves (unfavorably) to others.
· Comparing others unfavorably to ourselves.
· Doing what is unacceptable! (sin, addictions, bad habits) Get the help you need to stop these!

Because we as Christians have accepted Christ as our Savior, and recognize that we are all God's creations as well as new creations in Christ (2 Corinthians 12:9; Col.1:21, 22), we are called to accept ourselves and others as God does: unconditionally and lovingly. *"My grace is sufficient for you, for my power is made perfect in weakness." (2 Corinthians 12:9)* Grace is a central theme of our faith and a cornerstone of our acceptance through Christ.

What if we have not yet reached that level of self- and other-acceptance? As coaches, we see our clients as whole, creative, and brilliant, and increase their awareness and acceptance of themselves as that. How do we do this? By listening to the Holy Spirit, that still small voice. As coaches, we stand in for clients until they reclaim and accept who they fully are, as God's creations, including all their gifts and talents that honor God.

The value of being fully present, listening with one's whole being focused only on you, is a rare experience that cannot be underestimated. Also, knowing the energy required to make changes, we coaches encourage great self-care: spiritually, emotionally, and physically.

The need for honest feedback offered in love and acceptance contributes towards self-esteem. All clients should be able to count on this in the coaching relationship. In business and sometimes career or personal coaching, the coach can perform a 360-degree assessment where data is gathered from those who are in contact with the client in order to provide necessary feedback. This is done within the context of respect and acceptance. Honesty on both ends of the coaching relationship is essential in producing positive results. This is one of the advantages a coach has over a friend or an in-house mentor. As trained professionals, we are free from all other ties in providing objective, honest, supportive feedback. We can speak the truth in love without concern over how it will affect us personally or our business, working only in the client's best interest.

Liz and Jean

Liz and Jean both came to me, like many of my clients, in transition. Both had lost their jobs. We know that in our culture, with its emphasis on performance and appearance, that losing your job can be quite a blow to your self-esteem. The definition of self-esteem that some mental health professionals use includes:

- Having clear beliefs and values, and living them (integrity)
- Having a clear life plan
- Being connected with family

· Intimacy with others: listening, suspended judgment.

Liz had the advantage of being connected with a loving, supportive family and church family. According to research, people experiencing loss do best when they have a good support system. My role as Liz's coach was to provide unconditional acceptance and support, encouragement, and accountability as she searched for a new position. I also helped her to recognize and focus on her strengths, an especially important task because her former workplace had been eroding her view of her competence.

Of course, nothing happens in a vacuum, and Liz was also faced with planning her child's graduation party, catching up on things at home that had been neglected while working long hours in her stressful job, and working through the loss of the job with its resulting effect on her. So balance and self-care became additional coaching agendas. In the process of her renewal, she was able to see a family member in a new, more gracious light and make a positive shift in that relationship.

Liz was also able to shift from trying to please others constantly to seeing herself as pleasing God. Through our coaching, she learned the distinction between striving for excellence and perfectionism. Liz recognized she was her own harshest critic, and began defining for herself realistically what was enough. The messages she had heard in her head were, "You're not getting enough done", "you're not good enough." She identified these messages as not helpful, and not of God, and told them to get lost, while she responded with humor. *"Do not be conformed to this world but be transformed by the renewal of your mind, that you may prove what is the will of God, what is good and acceptable." (Romans 12:2).*

Liz learned to hold her expectations and goals "loosely", rather than tightly, trusting that as she did her part, so would God.

Clients may come looking for a career change and realize they need to make lifestyle changes first or during that process, like Liz did in making her devotional/quiet time a priority. Especially when someone is faced with making a decision they are not clear about, it's helpful to schedule extra quiet time. We find peace, contentment, and clarity in the presence of a loving God.

Jean had the additional challenge of being in recovery from an addiction. Also, she was under the care of a psychiatrist for depression, exploring church membership, and not part of a supportive family. As her coach, even with a mental health background, I did not deal with her depression or addiction because she was under the care of other professionals.

Through our coaching relationship, Jean established and put clear boundaries in place with her family so that they could not continue to take away from her sense of acceptance. She joined a church and developed a new "family" there. She started catching up financially and also cleared out the clutter in her home, both of which contributed to her feelings of success and acceptance. She began taking better care of her body and exercising more, which boosted her energy and self-image. Like Liz, Jean also benefited from focusing on her strengths and receiving my support, encouragement, and accountability.

"I realize I've sabotaged myself", she reported. I was able to give her loving, objective feedback, which resulted in her changing her behavior in job interviews, which resulted in a new position, which helped financially and contributed to her self-esteem. *"The truth will make you free." (John 8:32)*

Through the trusting, accepting relationship with a coach, the client is free to become all s/he was created to be. In addition to securing new jobs, through coaching both Liz and Jean made lifestyle changes which they will continue and which will help them to be the women God created them to be. They both also looked at their vision of God's plan for their lives and how to implement that plan. Despite their life circumstances, they radiated warmth, humor, and increasingly, joy and energy. They were a pleasure for me to work with. I look for a sense of humor and some energy in clients. I rejoice in celebrating their successes with them.

Besides coaching clients through career transition, how else is Christian acceptance practiced and achieved?

We can model and practice unconditional acceptance as parents, leaders, managers, and teachers. We all need loving, appropriate touch and words that reflect our true value. When we do not receive it, we find it difficult to give and can be caught in a vicious cycle which can extend for generations. As coaches we can be the enthusiastic, loving and accepting support for our clients.

Is our acceptance of others based on whether or not we approve of them, or whether they are Christians or not? I think not. We are called to love, not judge. We can accept and love all whom God puts on our path.

"We are all on the path from clueless to aware," said my first coach. I can find myself feeling irritated and impatient when people I've contracted with do not follow through in the way or time that they said they would. "Not everyone is as responsible as you, " reminds my mother. *"When I was a child, I spoke like a child, I thought like a child, I reasoned like a child; when I became a man, I gave up childish ways. For now we see in a mirror dimly, but then face to face." (I Corinthians 13:11, 12)* Just as parents expect different abilities from children at different ages, so we must remember that we and others are at different levels of development and adjust our expectations accordingly.

Some Christians who see themselves as having grown closer to Christ or become more Christ-like may forget that they have not always been at that level. *"For if you forgive men their trespasses, your heavenly Father also will forgive you;" (Matthew 6:14)* *"Judge not, that you be not judged. For with the judgment you pronounce you will be judged, and the measure you give will be the measure you get. Why do you see the speck that is in your brother's eye, but do not notice the log that is in your own eye? Or how can you say to your brother, 'Let me take the speck out of your eye,' when there is the log in your own eye? You hypocrite, first take the log out of your own eye, and then you will see clearly to take the speck out of your brother's eye." (Matthew 7: 1-5)*

To test how well you would respond in an unconditionally constructive or accepting way, you can visit my website and take the quiz found in the June 1999 Connections newsletter.

Coaching Moments

- What will fully accepting yourself look like?
- How can you be unconditionally constructive and accepting of others?
- What will you say about yourself after you fully accept yourself and others that you can't say now? How will you feel differently about yourself when you do?
- Who are you becoming in Christ?

Coaching Challenges

- As you pray this week, ask to see yourself and others through God's loving, accepting eyes.
- If this is a difficult area for you, get the help you need. If you need healing of past hurts that are keeping you from accepting yourself, get counseling. If you need help with addictions, get that help. If a clinical depression keeps you from accepting yourself, seek out a mental health professional. If you want the support, encouragement, accountability and focus of a coach as you go through a transition or want to fully discover and become the person God created you to be, contact me or one of the other coaches in this book, or check out www.ChristianCoachesNetwork.com.
- Oprah Winfrey has popularized the gratitude journal. Write down what you are grateful to God for about yourself in specific terms, like how He has created you: your mind, your eyes to see, your spiritual gifts, etc.

- Use your gratitude journal for writing about what you are thankful for in the people you have trouble accepting or relating to in a loving, accepting way.
- Recognize where judgmental thoughts are coming from, tell them to get lost, and ask God to replace them with loving, accepting thoughts.
- Write out some of the verses from this chapter on a card to remind you of your great worth as a child of God, a new creation in Christ. Refer to it frequently.

11 | GETTING YOUR LIFE BACK:

Unleashing Your Freedom Through Forgiving

By Judy McMaster Santos

Forgiving someone who has hurt you has all the appeal of a bad night's sleep. When someone has betrayed your trust, falsely accused you, said something cruel, damaged your reputation, stripped you of your dignity, or stolen your moment, it hurts. Any kind of physical, mental, spiritual, financial or emotional harm leaves bruises, sometimes deep ones. Nobody gets through this life unscathed.

Forgiving is as fundamental to the coaching process as it is to the Christian life.

We often resist forgiving, at least initially, feeling we are entitled to our anger. We feel victimized. We get defensive. Sometimes we feel so wounded by another's destructive behavior that we believe we can never trust or love again. Very often, we feel that the person who has caused the harm doesn't deserve to be forgiven.

Let's assume for a moment that the person who hurt you really doesn't deserve to be forgiven. It may well be true (although who among us does?). The truth is, we aren't doing the *other* person a favor by forgiving: We are doing *ourselves* a favor. The explanation is simple. We are not accountable for what other people do; we are responsible for what we do. And when we choose *not* to forgive, we are, in addition to disobeying God, allowing that person to drive our emotions – sometimes our life!

When you fail to forgive, you give your power away. Yes, really. As long as you choose to hold onto your pain, you are allowing the person who has harmed you to have control over your sense of who you are and interfere with your joy, your peace and perhaps even your willingness to love. Are you willing to be a volunteer victim to the one who has harmed you? To whom have you given your power? As long as you allow the person who has hurt you to drive your mood, you have relinquished your control to that person and given them permission to make you miserable. Often that control is evil, in that it finds a place between you and the Lord. What you have is the power to make choices about what comes into your life and what you allow to remain. If you are choosing God over all and allowing yourself some vulnerability in loving people, you can detach yourself emotionally or physically from someone who harms you. By doing this, you reclaim who you are in Christ and allow forgiveness to unlock the gate that traps and confines. Forgiveness is not an automatic response. It is a means to an end of misery.

The whole notion of deserving forgiveness is in dramatic contrast to what Christians know to be true. Jesus did it for us on the cross. I don't deserve to be forgiven, but He forgives me. And He forgives you. And any who ask.

"If we confess our sins, he is faithful and just to forgive us our sins and purify us from all unrighteousness."
    1 John 1:9

Time does not heal all wounds. Jesus does. Time only provides perspective. What we tend to do, instead of forgiving, is to put this hurtful situation out of our minds as much as possible. I speak of hurt, because anger is the layer that covers hurt.

Without forgiveness being addressed, we allow time to pass; and the incident gets stepped over, buried and (perhaps eventually), almost forgotten until something triggers the memory, re-opening a floodgate of emotion. But instead of going away, it settles in a murky pool deep within us, developing a root of bitterness and cynicism.

Un-forgiveness often gets in the way of God's healing and contributes to the destruction of human relationships, not to mention our relationship with God.

"Get rid of all bitterness, rage and anger, brawling and slander, along with every form of malice. Be kind and compassionate to one another, forgiving each other, just as Christ God forgave you."
Ephesians 4:31-32

When a bee stings you, you can pull the stinger out, and it still hurts. However if the venom is not removed, it infects your whole body.

We tend to write our own rules, instead of aligning with the Word of God. Sometimes we believe that if the offender has suffered as much as we have, they perhaps deserve to be forgiven. So we are able to be quite gracious about it. Mutual suffering has a way of preventing us from feeling victimized.

If your car is hit by another vehicle and the driver immediately accepts responsibility and is at least as upset as you are, forgiveness comes easily. The reverse is also true.

Forgiving is not the same as making excuses for someone. We have all heard people say, "Oh, I'm sure he didn't mean that; he just has a lot on his mind." Or "She is very often critical of others, that's just her way." This is not the same as understanding someone's situation. Making excuses for someone does nothing to absolve your feelings and only invites more emotion to stack up, with your permission. There needs to be some conversation around such issues, as well as forgiving behavior.

John's Story

John hired me to coach him through the transition of a new job in a different state. He was feeling some conflict about uprooting his wife and children and leaving both extended family and a host of friends. He was experiencing self doubt in his ability to make good decisions. As we began to explore his decision making process around the move, John shared an experience that he saw was clouding his thinking.

Just a year before, his brother-in-law was strapped for cash and asked John for a loan so he could get his car fixed and pay his bills until he could find a job. John didn't have a lot of extra money but believed it was right to share what he had for someone in the family who was struggling. So he wrote out a check for $3,000, leaving only $500 in his savings account. Instead of finding work, however, his brother-in-law cashed the check and left the country. John believed his brother-in-law did this deliberately and that he knew it would have an adverse effect on others.

There weren't any excuses that made his brother-in-law's actions acceptable. Forgiveness did not come easily for John. He struggled with resentment and self blame. Forgiving, however, is forgiving the debt as well as the betrayal of trust, and letting it go. As I worked with John as his coach, he began to unveil the truth. While layers of anger and grieving are certainly appropriate, he will not be free of the results of this exploitation until he forgives.

As Christians, we sometimes buy into the notion that if we are quick to forgive, we qualify as spiritual giants. However forgiving is not an option for a Christian, but simply an act of obedience. God gave us all that we need to forgive – Jesus. We just need to be willing. While it seems easier to dismiss or neglect God's gift, accepting God's gift of Jesus is the important part of getting a real sense of who we are as children of God.

". . . Forgive and you will be forgiven."
   Luke 6:37c

"Bear with each other and forgive whatever grievances you may have against one another. Forgive as the Lord forgave you."
Colossians 3:13

* * *

My brother Barrie, from whom I have gleaned nuggets of wisdom over the years, sees forgiveness as a process rather like walking down a stairway. You begin at the top step by asking God to help you forgive, confessing that you don't feel like forgiving but would prefer to hold on to the sense of entitlement dictated by your feelings. But you do this, and recognize it as a simple act of obedience to the Lord. From there, step by step and day by day, as you continue to seek the Lord's help, the levels of forgiveness continue. This requires tenacity and a true commitment to forgive. When you finally reach that last step, you know that the sting has gone out of the memory; and you are free. Sometimes this takes longer than any of us care to admit.

Mary's Story

Mary was heartbroken when she found out that her husband had been unfaithful to her. For many reasons, they decided to stay together and try to work things out. Some time later, Mary told her husband that she had forgiven him. She had taken the first step, but never gone beyond that. This was evidenced by the fact that for years, every time they argued, she brought up the issue of the affair, going over each painful detail with great emotion.

When I began coaching Mary, she was looking for something she felt was missing in her life. As she told me about the affair that had almost ruined their marriage years before, she began to see that she was still harboring resentment about it that spilled into other parts of her life, robbing her of her joy.

Because she was willing to acknowledge this and prayerfully give her hurt and herself over to the Lord, she came to a point of complete forgiveness and freedom. The Lord has done amazing things through her life since that time. She got her joy back.

* * *

When you forgive, you don't necessarily totally forget the facts; but the emotion that accompanied them is gone, the details become foggy and you know you have let go.

So where do we draw the line as Christians? If we forgive and then have the opportunity to forgive the same person for the same thing over and over, isn't something terribly wrong? Of course! It is our responsibility to forgive seventy times seven, but it is not our responsibility to stay in the company of a person or a situation that is dangerous or damaging. There are people with evil intentions and no conscience. There are times and places when we must "*. . . be as shrewd as serpents and innocent as doves*". *(Matthew 10:16b)*

Revenge is the opposite of forgiveness and has no place in the heart of a believer. Instead of utilizing the God-given ability to forgive, we attempt to play God by paying back wrong with wrong. *"Do not take revenge, my friends, but leave room for God's wrath. For it is written: 'It is mine to avenge; I will repay,' says the Lord."* *(Romans 12:17, 21)*

People who harbor grudges are not very pleasant to be around. They have a cynical view of life and the world and a repressed anger that sometimes seeks revenge. Pity parties attract those with similar attitudes who only feed on discontent and nurture the justification of their attitude. Whiners attract only whiners.

There is only one unforgivable sin. And that has nothing to do with what someone else has done to you.". . . *Every sin and blasphemy will be forgiven men, but the blasphemy against the Spirit will not be forgiven, either in this age or in the age to come."*

(Matthew 12:32-32)

While we wring our hands over the moral decay of society, the personal sin of un-forgiveness lurks, causing more damage to our spirit than we can comprehend.

As we take those bold steps to search our hearts and ask God to show us what spiritual housecleaning is required, we are embarking on an adventure with the Lord like no other. Claim your freedom in Christ and release the layers that may be holding you in bondage!

Coaching Moments

- As you pray this week, are you willing to ask the Lord to bring to mind any un-forgiveness that you have in your heart?
- As people and situations come to mind, will you ask God to help you in that process?
- Would it be helpful for you to journal this adventure?
- Are you punishing yourself for things you have done to hurt others?
- Do you need to forgive yourself? When are you going to do that?
- How will you feel when you have completely forgiven the people who have hurt you?

Coaching Challenges

- Create a new file on your computer or start a notebook and write down the names of all the people who have made an imprint in your life. Include your spouse, children, parents, siblings, in-laws, friends, colleagues, supervisors, teachers, people in church, former love relationships and that second cousin. Under each name, write down things that disappointed you, hurt your feelings, failed to meet your expectations, or in some way had a negative impact on you and then, how that made you feel. For example, you might write down: "Former Fiancé – left me at the altar. Felt abandoned, betrayed, disappointed, and humiliated."

· Leave yourself room to add to this list as the Lord brings other things to mind. You may be surprised how long this list becomes. You may even be embarrassed at the volume of your spiritual baggage.

· Commit all of this to the Lord in prayer and ask that you be given the help you need to forgive every person for every item on your list. If you have some big "stuff" on your list, you may not feel ready yet to let go. Confess your feelings to the Lord, adding that it is the desire of your heart to be obedient and forgiving. Ask for help in letting go.

· Come back to your list as more things/people come to mind to be added.

· Pray that God will bless (yes, that's *bless*) each person on your list, "*. . . Pray for those who persecute you . . . .*" *(Matthew 5:44)* (Yes, you may have to ask that He will help you to mean it!) Then ask the Lord to give you a fresh perspective, melting down whatever barriers of your heart that may have become crusty. *"Create in me a pure heart, oh God, and renew a steadfast spirit within me. (Psalm 51:10)* Keep at this, every day. You will find some things disappearing from your emotionally charged list quickly; others will take more time. *"Keep no record of wrongs." (Psalm 130:3)* Delete as you go. It may not take long to forgive the person who publicly embarrassed you by pointing out your shoe size in the seventh grade, but it may take a while to forgive the person who prevented you from getting a promotion last month. Just make sure you are really letting this go through the process of forgiveness, not making excuses or rationalizing someone's behavior.

- Keep forgiveness current so you aren't letting things stack up. Let this process be a part of your lifestyle so that when someone causes you harm, you immediately take it to the Lord (with all your feelings) and stay with the process.
- As this project nears completion, be willing to take a bold step and write down a list of things that YOU may have done that wronged others. Follow the same procedure, asking God to forgive you and to help you accept that forgiveness. Then, as appropriate (and only as appropriate), ask those you may have hurt or harmed to forgive you.

12 | THE JOY OF COMMUNITY

By Timothy E. Ursiny, Ph.D.

"Be completely humble, gentle, and patient always. Show your love by being helpful to one another. Do your best to preserve the unity, which the Spirit gives, by the peace that binds you together. There is one body and one Spirit, just as there is one hope to which God has called you."
Ephesians 4:2-4

He was a family man and a believer and had reached a level of success in his career that he never expected. He enjoyed the respect of his peers and felt the blessings of God in almost every area of his life. A humble man would respond with incredible gratitude and appreciation. He responded with ego and forgetfulness. He forgot who was in charge of his life. He forgot who was king. He forgot that he was just another sinner on the journey that this life brings.

Ironically, the man had been reading a book years earlier in which the author admitted to a specific sin that this man found horrible and incomprehensible. In pride, the man put down the book. Surely he couldn't learn anything from someone who could fall so badly (pride that cometh before the downfall). It wasn't but a year later that the man fell in a way identical to this "horribly sinful" author.

It took over a year for the man to come forward with his sin. The reasons he finally owned up to his wrongdoing were complex; the consequences were appropriately severe. Many losses occurred for him and his family. He lost his title, friends, the respect of colleagues, and ultimately, his career. He even had difficulty getting another job, because he felt that he needed to be honest about being fired from his previous employment for unethical behavior. He experienced humiliation due to fleeting publicity around his actions. He felt shamed by the frightened and crushed look in his wife's eyes as she tried to grapple with the losses. He felt like a leper and expected others to reject his worth as a human being. Some met his expectations and viewed him as beneath them, but not everyone related to him in the same way. In the end, there were three groups of people who reacted to his behavior from the previous year.

1. Some people judged him as unworthy and rejected his friendship.
2. Others tried to decrease his shame by attempting to diminish the seriousness of his sin.
3. A third group confronted him on or acknowledged the seriousness of his behavior, yet made sure that the man knew that God's grace covered his sin and more.

The only reason that the man survived the consequences of his actions as a better man was because of God's using his community in the third way: a community that spoke the truth in love. A community that hated the sin but loved the sinner. A community that came to the aid of a hurting family, bearing the love and grace of our Savior.

I know a lot about this man, because I *am* that prideful man who failed so badly. The event that I am writing about changed my life and my whole view on community. To share more details would be exhibitionistic on my part and detract from the main point. The main point is that God's community has incredible power. Many people have tried to give me credit for how I have rebounded from such hard times. The honest truth is that without the loving and wonderful community with which God surrounded me, I could very well be living in shame and isolation or complete separation from my Lord.

Community is an age-old concept. God created Eve because Adam was incomplete in and of himself. The people of Israel certainly were led by the Lord to live in a state of community. Today community can refer to your neighborhood, or to your church, or even to your small group within the church.

Some people in our present age get their sense of community in chat rooms on the Internet; others from coffeehouses where they talk with friends while sipping Latté. We yearn for community. Television shows like *Friends* and, even earlier, *Cheers*, show groups of people where "everyone knows your name" or who proclaim "I'll be there for you". The American public eats this message up because we all know deep down that we need others.

So where does coaching come in to all of this? Coaching is centered in being the person that God has meant you to be (thus one who does not live in isolation, but in relationship to God and others). Coaching focuses on helping people impact others (e.g., their community) for the positive. When we coach others, we have to remember that they do not live in a vacuum, but rather live in connection with other human beings. While coaching, the coach should never lose sight of the fact that when someone changes something in his or her life, they most likely are impacting someone else in the world in some way also.

Figure 10:1 contains an example of one form of a balance wheel that is often used in a coaching session. As you can see, many of the areas can be related to community depending on how you define the term.

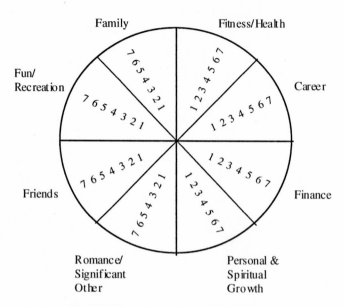

Figure 10: Life Balance Wheel: (7 = Completely satisfied; 1 = Completely dissatisfied). Within each of the areas, circle the number that best represents your level of satisfaction in that area of your life Then connect the dots. Imagine how your car would travel if the wheels were in this shape!

The well-balanced person is aware of how he or she impacts the lives of others. The self-aware person who is connected with the Holy Spirit has a focus on loving others and contributing to the welfare of the less fortunate.

When I used to practice therapy, I had a client who was furious at a church that would not give him money when he was hit with a financial crisis. He stood in lofty judgment of the "hypocrites" in the church and how they should have helped him. Regardless of what the church should or should not have done, what I found so intriguing about this gentleman is that he never once in his life gave money to a church or any charity. In other words, the community existed to serve him; but he did not exist to serve the community. This is not how God intended us to be. Effective coaching helps people see themselves clearly and assess to what level their contribution to their community is consistent with what they truly believe.

Being the son of a pastor and from coaching many ministers, I have heard many stories about people leaving the church because they didn't feel "a part of" the community. Now churches certainly need to create inviting environments that are friendly and embracing to new people. But individuals attending a church also have to take responsibility for connecting with others. Many times the people who don't feel embraced by the church have never attended Sunday School or joined a small group. Often these are *the* forms of community within a church, since the worship service is focused more on glorifying God. In coaching, people who are dissatisfied in their relationships are encouraged to develop specific plans to connect with others in an effective and proactive manner. Coaching helps people take responsibility for getting what they want rather than blaming others (or even the church) when they don't have it.

My wife and I are blessed to be part of a small group that we started through our church. We call the group a "Marriage Accountability Group". Basically it consists of five couples who meet two or three times a month to create a community focused on honoring and accountability. We share in each meeting where we have been selfish in our marriages and describe times when we felt honored by our spouses. Our group is dedicated to building solid marriages through authenticity, communication, support, challenge, offering observations, prayer, and accountability. In the truest sense of the word, we coach each other on our marriages. No one in the group pretends to have it all together when it comes to relationships, but we ask each other powerful questions and keep each other focused on the goal of having marriages of excellence. The experience of the group is awesome and life changing. It is coaching at its finest hour.

I hope that you have something in your life similar to the

community that we have found in this group. If you don't, consider the following questions and challenges.

Coaching Moments

- Whom do you consider as part of your community?
- When do you experience the most fulfilling sense of community?
- How specifically do you contribute to your community?
- What is the balance between what you receive from your community and how much you give?
- How well do you allow others to care for you? Name a time recently when you allowed someone to feel good about him or herself by accepting help from them.

Coaching Challenges

- What is one thing that you have always wanted to do for someone but have never done? What has kept you from doing it? When will you do it?
- Name three things that you can do to increase the sense of community among your friends and family? How and when will you implement these?
- Name someone you know that probably does not feel embraced by others in your specific community. What can you do to make them feel a part of the community and feel cared for? When and how will you show care to them?
- Do the balance wheel found in Figure 10. Are you satisfied with the results? If not, form a plan to move your scores to 6's and 7's.

Conclusion

If you are not a part of a genuine and loving community, I urge you to reach out to others. Join a church. Join a small group. Invite others over for dinner. Form a community and give to them. Give to them for the pure joy of it. In addition, let them give to you, especially if you are hurting and falling away from the Lord. I know I did and I thank God for the loving people who helped bring me back to Him.

By the way, I have since called and met several times with the author whom I judged so harshly. He is a wonderful, giving Christian man who is impacting the lives of men and women in a way that must please our Lord. He accepted my apology for thinking I was better than him and for judging him. He and I are in community.

Appendix A

CHARACTERISTICS OF AN EFFECTIVE SPIRITUAL COACH

By L. Cecile Adams

CHARACTERISTICS OF AN EFFECTIVE SPIRITUAL COACH

Affirms	Is Grace-full
Asks Questions	Is Objective
Assists in Planning	Leads
Assists in Skill Development	Listens
Bears God's Light	Points the Way
Celebrates	Possesses Self-Knowledge
Challenges	Practices the Spiritual
Clarifies	Disciplines
Creates Balance	Provides Connections
Encourages	Provides Feedback
Envisions	Reconciles
Evaluates	Seeks Truth
Guides	Shapes
Has Integrity	Shares Wisdom
Heals	Speaks Truth
Hears with the Heart	Strategizes
Is Caring	Supports Healthy Relationships
Is Confident	Values Learning
Is Faith-full	

Appendix B
CHRISTIAN COACHES NETWORK

The Christian Coaches Network (CCN) is a group of people dedicated to providing professional coaching from a Christian perspective, and provides a free resource to those looking for a like-minded coach.

The CCN membership represents a number of denominations, theological perspectives, coaching specialties, and life experience. Members coach successful people to become more successful, and support them in living life according to their values. Christian coaches truly understand and support what is important to a Christian.

With the advent of specialized training programs specific to coaching skills, coaching has dramatically moved to impact businesses, personal lives and ministry. Forward thinking Christians, churches, para-church organizations, pastors and Christian leaders are reaping the benefits of coaching.

Visit the CCN web site, www.ChristianCoachesNetwork.com, to learn more about coaching and the Christian Coaches Network. Our member coaches work with Christians in all walks of life who are interested in using their potential, gifts and skills more effectively and finding more joy and a deeper peace, in the process. Explore the CCN Coach Referral Service to find a Christian coach who best matches you!

Members of the Christian Coaches Network agree to the following Code of Professional Conduct:

1. I hold myself accountable to the highest level of integrity, honoring Jesus Christ individually and corporately, in all my associations with clients and colleagues.

2. I will maintain complete confidentiality with my clients, within the confines of the law.

3. I will be clear with my clients about the nature of the coaching relationship, including structure, fees, refunds, expectations and guarantees.

4. I will never give a client's name to anyone, for any purpose, without express permission.

5. I will give credit where credit is due for materials supplied by other sources, respecting copyrights, trademarks and intellectual property.

6. I will judiciously avoid conflicts of interest. If any should arise, I shall, without delay, inform concerned parties of my position.

7. I will represent myself honestly and clearly to my clients, and coach only within my areas of expertise.

8. I will actively pursue well-being, wholeness, and continual learning in my own life.

9. I will refer a client to another coach if I am not within my area of expertise or comfort, so the client gets the best possible coaching.

10. I will honor my Christian values in my professional conduct, placing neither blame nor blemish on the name of Christ, the Christian Coaches Network or the coaching profession.

Appendix C
CCN BOOK CREW

L. Cecile Adams

L. Cecile Adams is the Director of Treutlen House, a residential facility for children and youth, located in South Georgia. She is also the Director of LeaderShape4Life, a company designed to help people become the leaders they want to be and create the future they want to live. She is a personal coach, consultant, educator, writer, and editor with extensive experience in many arenas of church life, both in The United Methodist Church and ecumenically. She works with clergy and laity, sometimes as teams and sometimes individually, as well as with persons in the non-profit area.

Cecile is certified in conflict mediation and is certified to lead the RealTime™ Coaching Seminar. She is also a certified trainer of trainers, teaching those who will teach others how to teach. Her coaching is based on values and behavioral style. She values helping persons succeed and finding a higher meaning in life. She particularly appreciates helping persons create harmony between what they believe, value, and do.

You may contact Cecile through her web site at: www.LeaderShape4Life.wsmcafe.com.

Carwin Dover

Carwin Dover is a Relationship Coach. He has twelve years experience as a Marriage and Family Counselor with a special interest in relationship systems at home and at work. Carwin coaches couples, individuals and groups to develop their most important relationships. In addition to his counseling experience, Carwin has eleven years in retail management and three years as owner of a retail store. His experience lends itself to both work and home situations.

A special interest of Carwin's is being a resource for clergy and their staff and congregations. He has worked extensively with the ELCA Lutheran Synod in Montana and is now available as a coach by phone for all Synods in the USA.

You may learn more about Carwin, his extensive experience and training, by visiting either of his web sites: www.MyCoachsWebsite.com or www.LutheranCoffeeBreak.com.

Carol Gerrish

Carol Gerrish, Professional Certified Coach, partners with professionals, managers and executives to design, embrace and enjoy lives of balance, meaning and reward. Through her coaching company, TransformingWork, high-achievers are motivated and encouraged to fully use their unique talents and gifts.

She has over 20 years executive and management experience with leading insurance companies and as a strategic planning and management consultant. Carol is committed to helping businesspeople achieve success without sacrificing their personal lives in the process. She particularly likes to help women find personal satisfaction in the middle of life's busy-ness.

Carol is a graduate of the CoachU training program. She is a Board Member of the Christian Coaches Network (CCN) and an active participant in the International Coach Federation (ICF) and the New Jersey Professional Coaches Association (NJPCA).

She also led the Habitat for Humanity Women Build/Governor's Build initiative in New Jersey.

You may contact Carol through her web site www.TransformingWork.com.

Brent and Pam King: Limelite Photography

Brent King is a professional photographer and owner of Limelite Photography in Sumter, SC. He and his lovely wife Pam joined the Book Crew at the end of the project, contributing the resources of their fully digital studio and their outstanding photographic talent to provide a professional and symbolic cover photo.

You may contact Brent and Pam at www.LimeliteOnLine.com.

Ruth Ledesma

Ruth Ledesma is an executive coach. She coaches men and women who are ready to succeed – however they may choose to define "success." Her qualifications stem from 25+ years of helping people with leadership, career choices, work & disability issues, personal and career development, relationships, written communication, public presentations, etc. She has coached friends, acquaintances and clients all her life as a gifted amateur. Now she coaches as a trained professional.

Through Ledesma Associates and its subsidiary, Sustainable Leadership Programs, Ruth and colleagues provide an array of services designed to foster the maximum development of men and women and the various kinds of communities to which they belong.

Ruth can be reached through her website at www.RuthLedesma.com.

Marilyn O'Hearne

For over 20 years, Marilyn has followed her mission of facilitating connections, learning and growth. In her professional life she has accomplished this through coaching, counseling, speaking, writing, leading seminars, teaching at Webster University, and serving as a career management consultant. Connecting with the field of coaching has been a dream come true for Marilyn. She is passionate about empowering others to identify and live their dreams.

Marilyn practices and models balance in her life by enjoying a wide network of family and friends, pursuing valued interests and self-care, and being active in her church and community. Marilyn has lived in Brazil and Spain, is a member of the International Coach Federation, and has completed a thirty-hour program at the Summer Institute for Intercultural Communication as well as her coaching training.

You may contact Marilyn through her web site www.ConnectionsCoaching.com.

Terry L. Phillips

Terry is a Personal and Business Development Coach. He has been the licensee for Coach U in Asia since 1998, training coaches and moving the cause of coaching forward in the region.

After 14 years as a Pastor in the U.S. Terry and his wife Rose moved to Asia as missionaries in 1980. They have served in Indonesia and Malaysia and in 1989 moved to Singapore where he founded MTS Asia. (Missionary Tentmakers Serving Asia)

Terry is a Certified Behavioural Consultant and a Certified Coach Facilitator with Corporate CoachU International. He has a double major of Intercultural Communications and Leadership Development in graduate studies in Fuller School of World Missions and is certified in Whole Brain Technology.

You may contact Terry through the MTS Asia Pte Ltd. web site, www.MTSAsia.com.sg.

Judy McMaster Santos

Judy Santos works with people who want to make a difference. With strong conviction, unlimited ideas, big vision and a pragmatic nature, she weaves creative development together with private coaching, facilitating phone forums and training new coaches. She may be contacted through her website at www.JudySantos.com.

Judy is the Founder and Director of the Christian Coaches Network, which is a resource for Christians in search of a Christian Coach, and a value packed professional organization for it's members. Visit www.ChristianCoachesNetwork.com.

She is also the co-founder of Key Coaching Solutions, a collaborative enterprise that meshes creative development and coaching to Christian Boards and Leaders. To learn more visit www.KeyCoachingSolutions.com.

Judy is an award winning writer and publisher, who lives in the magnificent Pacific Northwest.

Timothy E. Ursiny, Ph.D.

Timothy E. Ursiny, Ph.D., the founder and president of Advantage Coaching and Training, is a success coach specializing in aiding corporations to develop their managers and executives to their fullest potential. Areas of expertise include communication skills, time mastery, conflict resolution, coaching skills, increasing productivity, eliminating stress, and finding balance in life.

Tim received his undergraduate degree in psychology from Wheaton College and his doctorate from Northern Illinois University. He is a member of the International Coaching Federation, the Chicagoland Chapter of the American Society of Training and Development, and the National Association of Business Coaches.

He has coached and trained coaches at such organizations as ServiceMaster, Arthur Andersen, Terminex, Ameritech, Andersen Worldwide, Sourcebooks, Old Navy and other quality organizations.

You may contact Tim at www.AdvantageCoaching.com.

Gary Wood

Gary Wood is President of G.E. Wood and Associates and co-founder of Key Coaching Solutions. He is a private, executive coach to Christian business owners, executives and leaders. Key Coaching Solutions provides executive level individuals, boards of directors and teams with individual and group coaching, facilitation, distance phone forums, round tables and creative development.

Gary and his wife Alice have been enthusiastic contributors and leaders within the Christian community for many years. Gary serves an international clientele by phone, from his home in the beautiful Muskoka region of Ontario, Canada.

To find out more about Gary and his practice, visit www.KeyCoachingSolutions.com.

Appendix D
COACHING RESOURCES

International Coach Federation

The International Coach Federation (ICF) is a non-profit, professional organization of personal and business coaches. The ICF provides a Coach Referral Service for those wishing to hire a coach who is a member of this organization. Among a number of benefits to the coaching profession and its members, the ICF accredits coach training programs and provides professional coach certification.

Learn more about ICF at their web site: www.CoachFederation.org.

Coach Inc.com

Coach Inc.com is the umbrella organization for a number of coaching-related services. These include the following and may be contacted through their web sites:

- **Coach U:** Coach Training (Includes a Coach Referral Service). www.coachu.com
- **Corporate Coach U:** Corporate Coach Training. www.ccui.com
- **Corporate Coaches, Inc.:** Coaching Services. www.corporatecoaches.com

- **Coach Live:** Coaching Events. www.coachulive.com
- **Teleclass.com:** Public Classes. www.teleclass.com

Therapist University

Founded by Dr. Patrick Williams in 1998, Therapist University is an organization dedicated to providing the programs, opportunities, and resources to help therapists have successful practices. The Institute for Life Coach Training is the main program of Therapist U, helping training professionals to add Life Coaching to their professional offerings. Patrick's personal mission is to "profoundly impact the lives of those he coaches and trains so that they may profoundly impact the lives of others." Through Therapist University, Patrick hopes to provide therapists and coaches with the skills they need to enrich their lives and the lives of their clients through Life Coaching.

Learn more about Therapist U at www.TherapistU.com.

Printed in the United States
1539400005B/208-213